SCOTTISH TRIALS

Noteworthy and Sensational Scottish Trials

AMY MATHIESON

WAVERLEY BOOKS

Published 2016 by Waverley Books an imprint of
The Gresham Publishing Company Ltd, Academy Park,
Building 4000, Gower Street, Glasgow, G51 1PR, Scotland
www.waverley-books.co.uk
info@waverley-books.co.uk
Find us on ☐ facebook/pages/waverleybooks

Copyright © 2016 The Gresham Publishing Company Ltd

Chapter 12 'Oscar Slater (1909)', originally appeared in
Scottish Murders published by Waverley Books.

ISBN 978 1 84934 172 1

Printed and bound in the EU

Contents

Introduction   5

1 Mary, Queen of Scots (1586)   15

2 Charles I (1649)   27

3 Captain William Kidd (1701)   40

4 Joseph Knight (1774, 1777–78)   53

5 'Deacon' Brodie (1788)   65

6 Thomas Muir (1793)   78

7 Sir Gregor MacGregor (1826)   90

8 William Burke (1828)   102

9 Madeleine Smith (1857)   112

10 Jessie McLachlan (1862)   125

11 The City of Glasgow Bankers (1878)   139

12 Oscar Slater (1909)   151

13 Helen Duncan (1944)   180

Bibliography   191

Introduction

What makes some trials more interesting than others? What makes a trial sensational? Is it the nature of the crime? The verdict of the court? The individual in the dock? Or the fact that it holds Scots law up to question in some way?

The thirteen cases explored in this book are not so much stories of crimes committed, as stories of the trials themselves: how the accused conducted themselves, how the prosecution argued its case. Scottish trials are not only famous for putting murderers in the dock. From financial scandals and 'the most audacious fraud in history' to high treason, piracy, witchcraft and sedition, *Scottish Trials* goes beyond some of the most notorious crimes ever committed to describe their legal consequences. In this book we examine some of the most famous cases to be tried in Scotland under Scots law, as well as looking at those which took place beyond Scotland's borders but which involved Scots, and some which became infamous because of the nature of the crime committed, or the person charged. The defendants in this book come from the high and the low of Scottish society, from kings to cabinet-makers, from noblemen to servants.

Scotland's unique legal system allows for three possible verdicts ('guilty', 'not guilty' and 'not proven') and throws up fascinating historical anomalies, as in the trial of Madeleine Smith for the murder of her lover in 1857, and its notorious 'not proven' verdict. When Scotland joined with England, Ireland and Wales in the Act of Union in 1707, this also brought it into contact with greater political issues, as in the trial of Thomas Muir for sedition in 1793. But the legal systems of other countries have played a part too, as with the case of Sir Gregor MacGregor's trial in France for the fraudulent 'Poyais' scheme. With its echoes of the Darien disaster, this scheme saw people buying fictitious rights to foreign territory and dying in the attempt to build new lives there.

Sometimes it is the importance of the person in the dock that makes a trial sensational and it is hard to think of a more notorious, or more important, figure than Mary, Queen of Scots. She was the first monarch on a Scottish throne to be charged with treason for her part in what became known as the 'Babington Plot' against her cousin Elizabeth I. Her trial began in October of 1586 and lasted only a few days, during which she defended herself with force and intelligence against those who accused her of conspiring with the plotters to put herself on Elizabeth's throne. Elizabeth's delay in signing the execution order, after the inevitable 'guilty' verdict was established, is legendary, but so too is Mary's courageous conduct throughout the trial itself and at her execution, leading many to ask whether she was in fact 'guilty' as charged.

Her grandson, Charles I, would also stand trial in Westminster just over sixty years later, to become the first monarch on an English throne to be charged with treason. The stand-off between the 'divine right of kings', a doctrine of royal and political legitimacy in which both Mary and Charles believed, against the will of democracy, represented by Parliament, brought Charles to a sorry end. After many bloody battles between his 'Cavaliers' and the Parliamentarian 'Roundheads', Charles was captured, and his trial for 'high treason' began in January 1649. It lasted only a week, during which Charles refused, as King, to enter a plea. His silence was taken as evidence of guilt and he was beheaded shortly after the trial ended. Like his grandmother before him, he met his death with courage. Both these 'royal' trials are sensational because of the figures at the heart of them, but they also heralded new eras for their respective nations, so politically and socially their impact was enormous.

Other individuals have also achieved great notoriety, such as Captain William Kidd, the Dundee-born son of a sea captain. Charged with piracy and murder, his trials took place in 1701 during the 'golden age' of piracy on the high seas. After sailing the high seas as a privateer (a private person or ship authorised to attack foreign vessels in times of war), he turned to piracy, although marriage to a wealthy woman precludes the notion that he did so for money. In all likelihood, Kidd enjoyed the excitement of his life on the high seas but in 1699 he was finally caught and arraigned for trial in Boston, and then sent to England to stand trial there the following year. He was an uneducated man but smarter than he appeared at his trials, when he did his best to look like the innocent dupe of others. Sadly for him, he fooled no one. He was found 'guilty' and hanged for his crimes.

Sometimes, there is no fame at all attached to the individual defendant or claimant, but the legal process of their case helps to change an entire way of life, as in the case of Joseph Knight. He was sold as a slave to one John Wedderburn in Jamaica and brought to Scotland in 1769. In 1774 in Perth, Knight took his 'owner' to court, having first run away in order to declare his right to 'leave' Wedderburn's 'employment'. His case stretched far beyond his own personal circumstances, however. In support of his claim, it was argued that slavery was not recognised by Scots law and when he subsequently won his claim in 1778 it helped to pave the way for the end of slavery throughout the British Empire.

Sometimes, a trial simply catches the public imagination, as with the trial of 'Deacon' Brodie, a carpenter who went to the gallows for burglary and was hanged by a contraption of his own design. The fall of such an outwardly respectable figure captivated the residents of Edinburgh during the time of the Scottish Enlightenment, as they learned of the good deacon's secret life: his mistresses, his fondness for gaming and his drinking. Unable to fund the lifestyle he enjoyed so much, Brodie turned to burglary. As a cabinet-maker it was part of his job to install and repair locks and many wealthy Edinburgh property owners turned to him to manufacture special locks and keys to keep their possessions safe. Brodie simply copied his own designs and let himself into the properties when the owners were asleep. His trial in August 1788 lasted only twenty-one hours in spite of the number of witnesses called. He was sentenced to hang, protesting his innocence to the end in the hope that his once good name would save him.

A huge outpouring of public sympathy for the defendant or defendants can also allow a trial to take up a place in history. At the end of the eighteenth century, a group of men known as the 'Scottish Martyrs' were tried for sedition. They were headed by a Glasgow-born lawyer, Thomas Muir, a political reformer who supported the French Revolution and Thomas Paine's *The Rights of Man*. He was arrested and charged after speaking at a radicals' meeting, and his trial began in Edinburgh in August 1793. He conducted his own defence and gave a truly remarkable closing speech in his own defence and in defence of his friends, but he was found 'guilty' nonetheless and transported to Botany Bay in Australia. His fate, and that of his fellow political campaigners, so distressed Scots folk that in 1844 they commemorated Muir and his friends in a monument built in the Old Calton Cemetery on Calton Hill in Edinburgh.

Few murder trials are not sensational, but some stand out because of the particular wickedness of the crime or from a strong belief that justice has not been done. William Burke and William Hare were from Northern Ireland but they were working as labourers in Central Scotland in the early nineteenth century when they realised that by supplying dead bodies to Edinburgh University's medical department for dissection, they could make much more money than by labouring on the streets of Edinburgh. Alas, they went from supplying dead bodies to creating them, and were soon charged in December 1828 with the murder of three people. The trial underwent an interesting twist when Hare turned king's evidence and spoke for the Crown against his former friend. Burke's common-law wife was also accused but while he was found 'guilty' and subsequently hanged, her verdict was 'not proven' in a case that both terrorised and captivated the Scottish public.

Madeleine Smith was the 22-year-old daughter of a highly respected Glasgow architect, who resided in the city's fashionable Blythswood Square, when she was accused in 1857 of murdering her French lover, Emile L'Angelier, by poisoning him with arsenic. What really shocked Victorian society though were the love letters she had written to L'Angelier before she had broken off their affair, letters which were explicit and passionate and not the kind of thing expected of a young woman from such a respectable family. Did she poison L'Angelier because he threatened to publish her letters and so ruin her reputation? At her trial, not only the jury but also the public couldn't quite decide if she was guilty or not, and the notorious 'not proven' verdict, unique to Scots law, would ensure that the question was never satisfactorily settled, even to this day.

Just a few years after Madeleine Smith's trial, the trial of Jessie McLachlan, who was convicted of murdering her friend and fellow servant in 1862, would cause a huge sensation, not least because, in an unparalleled act, she denounced the chief witness for the Crown as the real culprit. A servant-woman, Jess McPherson, had been found bludgeoned to death in the home of her employers in Glasgow's prestigious Sandyford Place. Inverness-born McLachlan was charged with the murder of her friend, but at her trial she sensationally accused the elderly but lecherous and often drunken 87-year-old James Fleming, the father of McPherson's employer. Jessie was found 'guilty' and sentenced to hang but a Court Commission appointed to look into the case commuted this sentence to life imprisonment. Did they know something the rest of us didn't?

But the crime of murder does not have a monopoly on the sensational. Sir Gregor MacGregor, a descendant of Rob Roy MacGregor, was charged in 1826 with what one historian has called 'the most audacious crime in history'. He had sold pieces of a fictitious land in South America to people who then sailed off to work that land; few of them, sadly, survived the horrendous experience. Born near peaceful Loch Katrine, MacGregor's life was anything but peaceful: a former soldier, he had a colourful history, travelling to many different parts of the world and getting into various scrapes, many of them financial. His trial actually took place in France, and, rather sensationally, he was acquitted. The whole experience of being on trial didn't stop him spending the rest of his life trying to swindle more people out of their money using similar rotten schemes.

Another financial scandal provided for yet another sensational trial, this time in 1878 when one of Scotland's biggest banks, the City of Glasgow Bank, collapsed. More than six million pounds were lost, and as a team of financial regulators looked through the books, they discovered that most of it had been laundered by the bank's directors. Eight men, most of them from the richest parts of the city, were tried for fraud, falsehood and theft in a trial that was financially complex but shocking nonetheless. The men, former merchants who had been lining their own pockets with the bank's money, all received between eight and eighteen months in prison, despite the fact that many of them were elderly.

The trial of Oscar Slater in 1909 for the murder of Marion Gilchrist resulted in the defendant spending eighteen-and-a-half years in jail for a murder he did not commit thanks to over-zealous policing, a disregard for sound investigative procedure and undoubtedly social, religious and racial prejudice. Oscar Slater was born in Germany to a Jewish family and moved to London at the age of twenty-one. Far from being the perpetrator of a horrible crime he was the victim of a Scottish miscarriage of justice. The sensational part of this trial occurred nineteen years after it took place when Slater's conviction was finally quashed in 1928 thanks to the efforts of a large number of people who had become convinced of his innocence. These included

Detective-Lieutenant John Trench, who was suspended from duty because he refused to accept that Slater was guilty, and Sir Arthur Conan Doyle, one of a number of well-known men who helped achieve justice for Slater.

Oscar Slater was released from prison in November 1927 but on licence and without a pardon. In July 1928, the newly established Scottish Court of Criminal Appeal quashed Slater's conviction but did not grant him the pardon he so wanted. If Oscar Slater did not kill Marion Gilchrist all those years ago then someone got away with her murder but exactly who remains a mystery.

Occasionally, the times themselves dictate the sensational element of a trial: it was during the Second World War that a rather harmless medium from Callander, Helen Duncan, was charged with witchcraft. She had become popular after the First World War, when many turned to spiritualism in the wake of devastating loss. She conducted séances, during which ectoplasm (a gauze-like substance) would emerge from her mouth. In 1944, Duncan would be the last woman ever to be charged under the British Witchcraft Act of 1735 when one of her séances in November 1941 drew attention to the sinking of a British battleship, HMS *Barham*. The battleship had been sunk on 25 November 1941 by a German submarine with a loss of 841 lives. In an effort to conceal the sinking from the Germans and to protect British morale, the Admiralty had censored all news of *Barham*'s destruction. After a delay of several weeks the War Office notified next of kin but they added a special request for secrecy. The naval authorities had taken a special interest in Duncan thereafter and she was eventually arrested in 1944. Possibly they were worried that she might continue to reveal secret information, whatever the source. Tried in London, she was found 'guilty' of fraud, serving nine months in prison. Her conviction had one long-lasting effect: it almost certainly contributed to the repeal of the Witchcraft Act of 1735.

An individual's status, the audacity of the crime committed, the uniqueness of a verdict and a taste of the times, all of these go together to make up the 'sensational' aspects of a trial and help to make it live on in history. Even today, just as then, arguments will rage about the innocence or guilt of those tried, as with Mary, Queen of Scots, or Madeleine Smith.

Nonetheless, these trials get to the heart of who we are as human beings, because they call on individuals to defend themselves, their beliefs or their behaviour against often overwhelming odds. Even when we are sure they are guilty and even when we find their crimes repugnant, we still find their trials fascinating because of that moment when they are put centre stage and heard by all. Not all the trials in this book show the Scottish (or English or French) legal systems at their best, but they do show our willingness to give even the most wicked of criminals a chance to defend themselves.

Chapter 1

Mary, Queen of Scots (1586)

*'I am clear from all Crime against the Queen;
I have excited no Man against her, and I am
not to be charged but by mine own Word or
Writing, which cannot be produced against
me. Yet can I not deny but I have commended
myself and my Cause to foreign Princes.'*

BACKGROUND

Born in 1542 at Linlithgow Palace, Scotland, to King James V of Scotland and his French wife, Mary of Guise, Mary became Queen of Scots at only six days old when her father died shortly after the Battle of Solway Moss. Her wily mother came from a powerful French family, and when her daughter reached the age of five, she sent her to the court of Henri II in France along with her closest childhood friends, the 'Four Marys' (Mary Fleming, Mary Beaton, Mary Seton and Mary Livingston). In 1558, the same year that her cousin Elizabeth acceded to the English throne, Mary married Henri II's eldest son, Francois, the Dauphin of France. But the Dauphin was physically weak: he died two years later, only eighteen months after the death of his much-loved father. Mary no longer had a place at a French court ruled over by Catherine de Medici and her mad younger son, Charles; on 14 August 1561, she sailed for Scotland and her throne.

Some have suggested that Mary came back to Scotland with the English throne in her sights, although Mary herself always denied this. Nevertheless, she did refuse to ratify the Treaty of Edinburgh that recognised Elizabeth as Queen. Mary had her own claim to the English throne: her father was the son of James IV and Margaret Tudor, the sister of Henry VIII. To some, her claim was greater than Elizabeth's, who, as the daughter of Henry VIII and his second wife, Anne Boleyn, had been removed from the succession when her father beheaded her mother to marry his third wife, Jane Seymour. She had come to the throne only after the deaths of her father, her half-brother Edward VI, and her Catholic half-sister, Mary, commonly known as 'Bloody' Mary for her burning of Protestant martyrs. Elizabeth was a Protestant queen but she felt shaky on the throne, sensitive to others' claims, their greater popularity and the possibility of a Catholic uprising.

And her Catholic cousin across the border was indeed popular. She was young and very pretty, unusually tall and slim, with a natural grace as well as the refined manners of aristocratic France. Her pale skin was smooth, and her reddish brown hair fashionably curled. Even though she was a Catholic queen in a country going through the Reformation (a movement that would result in the establishment of the Protestant Church), her arrival in Scotland was hailed as a great occasion. From the beginning, Mary showed herself to be wise and tolerant, extending sympathy and understanding to those of both the Protestant and Catholic faiths. She showed every sign of taking after her clever mother, who had ruled in her stead while she was in France. To that end, she was even able to tolerate, and occasionally stand up to, the formidable firebrand preacher John Knox, the author of *The First Blast of the Trumpet Against the Monstrous Regiment of Women*. Inspired by the presence of Mary's mother on the Scottish throne, and her cousin, Mary Tudor on the English one, the book deplored the fact of women in positions of power.

This happy beginning to Mary's reign contrasted hugely with that of her cousin, Elizabeth. Elizabeth was forever resisting urgent requests to marry and frustrating her advisors with her tendency to parry and delay. Mary, on the other hand, was keen to marry and strengthen alliances. Scotland was a much more fragmented country than England, and she showed a strong hand in keeping different members of the Scottish aristocracy on side. But it was hard work doing it alone, and she knew a supportive partner would help her. Her problem was, who to choose? Lord Henry Darnley seemed to be a very good catch and one who could actually enhance her own claim to the English throne, should she ever wish to make it. He was the son of Lady Margaret Douglas and the Earl of Lennox. Margaret herself was the daughter of Henry VIII's sister, Margaret Tudor, Mary's own grandmother. Darnley's father, the Earl, could also trace his family back to aristocratic roots, to James II of Scotland. Thus, Darnley had his own connections to both the English and Scottish thrones.

It might have seemed the perfect match on paper, but Darnley soon showed his true colours after his marriage to Mary in July 1565. Her second marriage would prove worse than her first, for Darnley was a weak, vicious man, paranoid and jealous of his wife's friendship with an Italian singer at her court, David Rizzio. Mary's enemies preyed on Darnley's insecurities until one night in March 1566, drunk and violent, he broke into the queen's private chambers where she was dining with Rizzio. Darnley's friends dragged the screaming Rizzio away and stabbed him to death. It was a brutal sign that Mary's power was seriously on the wane. Just three months later, she gave birth to her son, James.

But Lord Darnley was not to live to see his son grow up and ascend the throne: in February 1567 he died at Kirk o'Field in extremely suspicious circumstances. An explosion had gone off at the Old Provost's Lodging, where Darnley was staying, completely destroying the building. Darnley's body, however, was found further away, over the town wall that surrounded the structure. It appeared that he had been strangled. The Sheriff of Edinburgh, James, the fourth Earl of Bothwell, soon came under suspicion for the death and within months was being publicly accused. Mary's reluctance to pursue these accusations and have Bothwell arrested only fanned the flames.' Rumours began that Bothwell and Mary were, in fact, having an affair.

Bothwell did stand trial for Darnley's death in April in a prosecution brought by Darnley's father but after eight hours he was found 'not guilty'. Later in April Mary set out from Stirling Castle, where she had been visiting her baby son, for Edinburgh. Bothwell intercepted her party and escorted her to Dunbar Castle, for her own safety he said. It was at Dunbar, claimed Sir James Melville, one of Mary's retinue, that Bothwell raped the queen. Within days, however, Mary signed a statement declaring she had been neither abducted nor raped by Bothwell, and on 15 May she married him. There were no celebrations, and now Bothwell's enemies were up in arms. He was eventually exiled to Denmark and Mary herself imprisoned in Loch Leven Castle. She escaped in May 1568 but her forces were defeated at the Battle of Langside. She fled south to England, the land of probably her greatest enemy.

Mary wrote to Elizabeth many times, requesting a meeting with her, but her cousin always refused and the two queens never met. Instead, Mary was held prisoner in a series of castles over the next eighteen years, until her final residence at Fotheringay.

TRIAL

Anthony Babington and his associates had been planning

the assassination of Protestant Elizabeth and the accession of Mary as a Catholic queen. Their confessions, as well as admissions of Mary's own secretaries plus copies of incriminating letters, served to accuse Mary of complicity in their plot. She was arrested and taken to Fotheringay in the custody of Sir Amyas Paulet. A Commission of Inquiry was issued to the Archbishop of Canterbury and various other lords. It was alleged that Mary and others had 'engaged in conspiracy tending to Her Majesty's hurt' and the Commissioners were to hear evidence and give sentence. On 11 October 1586, they arrived at Fotheringay.

Mary issued her famous denial, quoted at the beginning of this chapter. The next day, she accepted her written statement as accurate but added that she did not enjoy the protection and benefit of the laws of England since she had come into England to crave aid, and had been detained ever since. Her denial of the authority of the Commissioners caused trouble and some of them came to see her. She maintained her objection and said she would listen to their arguments against the objection but by way of interlocution and not judicially. These discussions appear to have lasted two days. She would, she said, answer in a full Parliament so that she might be declared next to the succession but 'to the judgement of mine adversaries among whom I know all defence of mine innocency will be barred, flatly, I will not submit myself.' In vain, they threatened to proceed in her absence, but eventually on 14 October, it was agreed that, if her protest were received but not accepted, she would appear 'being anxious to refute the charge.'

And so the Commissioners took their places according to an elaborate scheme and ceremonial that had been settled in advance. A chair had been placed on the dais for Queen Elizabeth who was not present. Mary's chair was in the middle opposite Elizabeth's. 'I am a Queen by right of birth and my place should be there under the dais,' she declared. She was denied counsel and papers as Mr Justice Gawdy opened for the prosecution, accusing her of knowing and approving of Babington's conspiracy, and of promising her assistance. She denied all of this and demanded production of her own writing to prove it. Extracts were read from Babington's confession; Mary replied that many letters had passed between her and many men but that didn't make her privy to all their wicked counsels.

Copies of her correspondence with Babington were read out. Babington wrote of armed rescue and the assassination of Elizabeth, words intended for 'the usurper, from obedience of whim by the excommunication of her we are made free, there be six noble gentlemen, all my private friends, who for the zeal they bear to the Catholic cause and Your Majesty's service will undertake the tragical execution.' Mary's reply was long and detailed, going to every point of the letter and contained the words 'By what means so the six gentlemen deliberate to proceed.'

Mary demanded her accusers prove she had ever

received Babington's letters. 'A packet of letters that had been kept from me almost a whole year came into my hands about that time but by whom sent I know not.' She maintained the detailed reply was not hers. Evidence from her secretaries was produced; Mary countered:

> 'The majesty and safety of all princes falleth to the ground if they depend upon the ways and testi-mony of secretaries. I am not to be convicted but by mine own word or writing. If they have written anything which may be hurtful to the Queen, my sister, they have written it altogether without my knowledge, and let them bear the punishment of their inconsiderate boldness.'

To the suggestion that 'she purposed to convey her title to the Kingdom of England to Spain', she replied that she had no kingdom to convey, but it was lawful for her to give these things which were hers at her pleas-ure and not be accountable for the same to any, as if it could be any possible concern to any Englishman that on Elizabeth's death he might be handed over to the mercy of Philip of Spain. Mary admitted her cipher and that she had used it for corresponding, but when she was pressed with the confessions of her secretaries she flatly denied the allegations, denying again that she knew Babington.

Towards the close of the day she was taxed with let-ters she had sent abroad praying for foreign aid. Her answers were significant – that such things 'made not to the destruction' of Elizabeth, and if foreigners laboured to set her at liberty it was not to be laid at her door. Moreover she had often informed the Queen she would seek her liberty.

The next day she renewed her protest, adding that the Commissioners were so misusing their powers as to bring into question the religion she professed, the immunity and majesty of foreign princes, and the private intercourse of princes. She also complained that she was made to descend from her royal dignity and appear as a party before a tribunal simply in order to be excluded from the succession, and said that she only appeared lest she should seem to have neglected the defence of her own honour and innocence, and quoted the accusation made against Elizabeth herself of complicity in Wyatt's rebellion. Finally, she asked for an advocate and that as a princess she might be believed upon her word; for, she added, 'it were extreme folly to stand to their judgement whom she saw most plainly to be armed with prejudice against her.' Burleigh answered that they were there merely to arrive at the truth. She interrupted that the fact could never be proved. The secretaries could never have confessed but out of fear of torments or hope of reward and impunity. She complained that her papers had been taken away and that her secretary was not there to assist her.

They then proceeded to read her letters and she again drew attention to her former secretaries: what they declared contrary to their duty to her could not be received; once forsworn they had lost credit. Finally, being pressed about the royal succession to Spain, she said she had been urged to establish the succession in Spain or in an English Catholic, and had incurred displeasure because she would not consent, 'but now, all my hope in England being desperate, I am fully resolved not to reject foreign aid.' Finally she asked to be heard in a full Parliament or to speak with the Queen and her Privy Council.

This ended the proceedings at Fotheringay and the Commission adjourned to the Star Chamber at Westminster where they reassembled on 25 October 1586. Mary was not present and the only business was to call her secretaries to establish the validity of, and copy, the letters supposedly written by Mary. Thereupon the Commissioners pronounced the charge against Mary to be true. Although the findings would only affect Mary herself, it was thought advisable to declare that the sentence in no way affected her son, King James. It was important to keep him from forming a personal grievance and active steps were now taken to prevent his taking up arms to rescue or avenge his mother. To his eternal disgrace, he contented himself with verbal remonstrances after her execution.

Parliament confirmed the sentence and then both Houses presented a humble Supplication to Elizabeth, desiring in stately language that Mary's execution should be decreed. Elizabeth's answer was evasive, and after twelve days she returned a final reply, which she herself described as an 'answer answerless'. Some would have it that Elizabeth's initial reluctance to sanction her cousin's execution was an elaborate pretence that actually concealed her complicity in the plot to have Mary put to death. Others see only the machinations of Elizabeth's advisors as they tried to trick her into consenting to her cousin's execution. Mary after all was a relative and of royal blood like herself and Elizabeth could have been experiencing genuine distress as she considered authorising Mary's death by execution. The Lord Chancellor and the Speaker then procured a royal audience to give their reasons why Parliament should adhere to their resolutions, despite the fact that Elizabeth had desired them to find another solution. Again, she declined to commit herself and dismissed Parliament. Meanwhile the diplomats were busy and the French Ambassador was especially active in his efforts to prevent the execution. Still Queen Elizabeth would not give a decisive answer. She even wrote to Amyas Paulet asking him to 'shorten' Mary's life and spare her the necessity of condemning her cousin to death, but he refused. After weeks of hesitation she eventually signed the warrant and Mary's execution was carried out on 8 February 1587.

EXECUTION

The execution itself was a touching scene with her ladies-in waiting sobbing hard. The story that her little dog hid itself in her skirts as she was killed affected many and passed into legend. Her sense of herself as a great queen lasted until the end but the many mysteries of her colourful life have done her image harm. Was she really a conspirator to murder, not just once with regard to her second husband Henry Darnley, but twice with regard to her cousin, Elizabeth? Or was she tragically wronged, the innocent victim of others' ruthless ambitions? Mary was not stupid or rash. She was popular in the early part of her reign, yet few tried seriously to rescue her during her long confinement. The truth is, Scotland no longer wanted or needed her, and she was a thorn in the flesh of England's paranoid Elizabeth I. Mary's trial shows her intelligence and her argument concerning her correspondence with Babington was correct – without concrete evidence written in her own hand, and proved to be her hand, she could not be convicted of anything. In subsequent years, the 'Casket Letters' (purporting to be letters in which she confessed her part in the murder of Darnley) would further damage her posthumous reputation, but as recent scholars have argued, these letters, which no longer exist, were almost certainly forgeries. It was a time of plots and plans and dark deeds, and Mary was at the very centre of them. Like many before her, indeed like Elizabeth's own mother, Anne Boleyn, she was not able to survive a barrage of trumped-up charges.

CHAPTER 2
Charles I (1649)

*'Then for the law of this land, I am no less
confident, that no learned lawyer will affirm
that an impeachment can lie against the King,
they all going in his name: and one of their
maxims is, that the King can do no wrong.'*

This was how Charles I defended himself at his trial.
He is the only king in British history ever to have been
charged, found 'guilty' of treason and subsequently
executed. His greatest failing was his belief in the divine
right of kings, while his people came to believe him
to be a despot and guilty of absolutism. When Oliver
Cromwell rose up against him and commanded the
New Model Army, the 'Roundheads', to fight against
Charles's soldiers, the 'Cavaliers', during the Civil War,
it was the first time a king was deposed by his own
people. It is still, today, a divisive moment in history. For
some, the trial and execution of a king represents one
of the most shameful episodes in British history; for
others, it was Britain's one and only chance to become
a republic and the only time it really loosened the grip
of royal rule.

BACKGROUND

Charles I was born on 19 November 1600 in Scotland, in Dunfermline Palace, but he was later moved to England at the age of four, after a sickly childhood. He wasn't intended to rule over England and Scotland at all: it was only when his elder brother, Henry, died in 1612 at the age of eighteen, that this second son of James VI of Scotland and I of England, who took over the succession on the death of Elizabeth I, became next in line to the throne. James's own mother was, of course, Mary Queen of Scots – a sad lineage that Charles should perhaps have paid heed to. His great-great-uncle was Henry VIII who was, like him, a second son not meant to be king. Henry only acceded to the throne when his elder brother, Arthur, died. Perhaps the accident of second sons making it to a destiny initially intended for another can be seen as a warning of tough times ahead, for both Henry VIII and Charles I are two of the most notorious rulers in British history.

Charles was very much a Stuart in the mould of his father and his grandmother, inheriting many of their traits and attitudes, and not all of them good ones. Both Mary and James believed absolutely in the divine right of kings – a belief that mistakenly convinced Mary that her cousin Elizabeth would never execute her, even though she kept her prisoner for nineteen years. Like his father, James, Charles also believed in the divine right of kings, but his beliefs went much further than this – he believed he could reign without Parliamentary approval because he was answerable only to God: 'Kings are not bound to give an account of their actions but to God alone.' The people did not matter; Parliament, with its democratically elected members (democracy as it was understood then – women and working-class men without property were not allowed to vote or to stand for Parliament) did not matter either.

His father, James, hadn't been the most popular of sovereigns, as many had found his ways high-handed and his manner unsympathetic. In 1605, he had survived an attempted assassination, which came in the form of the Gunpowder Plot. A conspiracy led by Robert Catesby to blow up the Houses of Parliament failed when Guy Fawkes, who placed the explosives, was arrested. The scheme reflected Catholic desperation after the failure of previous plots to remove James and the new sanctions he had imposed against Catholics. James had been brought up in the Protestant faith, and part of his anti-Catholic stance was a position he took up against his disgraced mother.

Charles didn't heed any of the warnings that these grisly matters involving his father and grandmother might have given him. He was more inclined towards Catholicism than his father, not having the shame of an executed mother to contend with and having been brought up by less rigid scholars. He controversially married the Catholic princess, Henrietta Maria of France, who was the sister of Louis XIII – controversial because, as part of the marriage agreement, she was permitted free exercise of the Catholic religion. She could pray and attend Mass, as she wished. After so short a time from the death of Elizabeth, who had burned Catholic martyrs at the stake, this was remarkable.

But more controversy was to follow: within the first four years of his reign, three Parliaments would be summoned and dissolved; and for eleven years he would rule without one at all. His reign was stormy and difficult from the beginning, in contrast to his marriage. The public Charles had an unsympathetic personality but in private he seems to have been quite different: his marriage appears to have been a happy one. Henrietta was no beauty but they loved one another, and she gave him seven children (although it is believed he fathered two children outside of wedlock). His eldest surviving son, Charles II, would return to the throne in 1660, during the Restoration and after the death of Oliver Cromwell, the Protector. But this was all a long way away from Charles I's reign.

Charles's particular religious convictions created trouble for him from the start. The union of Scotland, England and Wales was, as yet, mainly a royal one – the Act of Union would not come into being until 1707. Of all the religious divides, the most serious was between the Protestant and Catholic factions. Charles's preference for Catholicism made many London Parliamentarians nervous and his support for radical Catholics like Richard Montagu, whom he made a royal chaplain, made many more distrust him. He made unwise choices in his friends and even more so in his enemies. Further unpopular appointments, such as making the Duke of Buckingham, who had led a disastrous campaign against the Spanish, the new Chancellor of Cambridge University, didn't help. In 1626, the House of Commons launched this direct criticism:

> 'We protest before your Majesty and the whole world that until this great person [Buckingham] be removed from intermeddling with the great affairs of state, we are out of hope of any good success; and we do fear that any money we shall or can give will, through his misemployment, be turned rather to the hurt and prejudice of your kingdom.'

This criticism should have rung alarm bells in Charles's ears – Parliament was publicly admonishing him for his behaviour, and for his appointment of Buckingham. But he paid no attention, and refused to dismiss his friend. Instead, he dismissed Parliament. It caused outrage, and on 23 August 1628, Buckingham was assassinated.

Charles still didn't heed the warnings. He went ahead with his plans, no matter how unpopular they were. His aim was to impose new religious practices and regulations, but he also wanted to change laws in both England and Scotland. The Presbyterians in Scotland resisted, however – they refused to acknowledge the new *Book of Common Prayer* that Charles had installed in all churches throughout the country. They suspected Charles of trying to anglicise the Scottish church. The Covenanters, a group of nobles who refused to follow the new rules, rose up against him, but Charles put down their rebellion in a bloody and brutal manner at Berwick. Many Covenanters were forced to flee abroad or go into hiding.

But Charles wasn't finished. In 1640, he raised an army in Ireland and weakened the Irish Parliament's power. The Scottish government declared itself independent of the King in response, and the Earl of Montrose successfully led an army against Charles at Newburn, much to the Covenanters' delight. After this humiliation, Charles couldn't command his armies with anything like the same authority. It was the Parliamentarians' chance, and they took it. Parliament brought in a series of measures, the most important of which was 'The Protestation'. This attacked the 'wicked counsels' of Charles's government. It promised to defend 'the true reformed religion', that is to say, Protestantism, as well as Parliament itself and the king's person, honour and estate. In spite of all this, Charles improved his own military position that summer by securing the favour of the Scots with the promise of the official establishment of Presbyterianism. In return, he was able to enlist considerable anti-Parliamentary support.

He needed it. In 1641, the Irish rose up against him. They argued that Charles had been led astray by the malign influences of other men. The transfer of land between Catholics and Protestants enflamed passions there and Charles struggled to hold onto power. The Irish Catholic army professed their loyalty to the King by massacring Protestants, much to the English Parliament's horror. They did not trust Charles's motivations when he called for funds to put down the Irish rebellion. Many members of the House of Commons feared that forces raised by Charles might later be used against Parliament itself.

It almost happened. In 1642, the first English Civil War began, after Parliament seized London and Charles was forced to leave the capital. Parliament remained in control of London, the south-east and East Anglia. Charles first raised his royal standard in Nottingham then he moved to Shrewsbury before setting up court at Oxford. The Battle of Edgehill on 23 October 1642 was the first pitched battle of the war but the outcome was inconclusive. Charles's Royalist Army was, however, defeated by the Parliamentarian New Model Army at the Battle of Naseby on 14 June 1645 and this defeat signalled many more for the Royalists. Charles escaped from the Siege of Oxford and ultimately surrendered to the Scots at Newark. Having little love for a Scots-born king who had never visited his own country as an adult, they were only too happy to deliver him to Parliament in 1647. He was imprisoned at Holdenby House in Northamptonshire until he was taken to Newmarket by the New Model Army.

By this time mutual suspicion had developed between

the New Model Army and Parliament, and Charles was eager to exploit it. He tried to escape to the Isle of Wight but was detained at Carisbrooke Castle. His attempts at duplicity in further bargaining just irritated his opponents more, however, and added to the public perception of him as a man that couldn't be trusted. After all, Charles didn't believe that he had to negotiate at all: he believed in the divine right of kings; his will was stronger than Parliament's – why should he have to bargain for his position?

His unwillingness to see that a king only rules for as long as the people are with him was possibly Charles's biggest mistake. He thought he could still hold sway, and tried to trick his jailors, signing a secret treaty with the Scots while in prison that they would invade England on his behalf and restore him to the throne. Their invasion precipitated the Second Civil War. The defeat of the Scots forces at Preston in August 1648 ended Charles's chances for good. He was arrested and charged with treason.

TRIAL

A special court was created for Charles's trial. After the First Civil War, the Parliamentarians accepted the premise that the King, although wrong, had been able to justify his fight, and that he would still be entitled to limited powers as regal head under a new consti-tutional settlement. It was now felt that by provoking the Second Civil War even while defeated and in captivity, Charles showed himself responsible for unjustifiable bloodshed. The secret treaty with the Scots was considered particularly unpardonable. 'A more prodigious treason,' said Cromwell, 'than any that had been perfected before; because the former quarrel was that Englishmen might rule over one another; this to vassalise us to a foreign nation.' Cromwell had, up until this point, supported negotiations with the king, but he now rejected further diplomacy.

No English king had ever been tried before. Charles was accused of treason against England by using his power to pursue his personal interest rather than for the good of the country. The charge against Charles I stated that the King, 'for accomplishment of such his designs, and for the protecting of himself and his adherents in his and their wicked practices, to the same ends hath traitorously and maliciously levied war against the present Parliament, and the people therein represented ...'; that the 'wicked designs, wars, and evil practices of him, the said Charles Stuart, have been, and are carried on for the advancement and upholding of a personal interest of will, power, and pretended prerogative to himself and his family, against the public interest, common right, liberty, justice, and peace of the people of this nation.'

Estimated deaths from the first two English Civil Wars are reported as 84,830 killed with estimates of another 100,000 dying from war-related disease; this out of a population of only 5.1 million. The indictment against the King therefore held him 'guilty of all the treasons, murders, rapines, burnings, spoils, desolations, damages and mischiefs to this nation, acted and committed in the said wars, or occasioned thereby.'

The High Court of Justice consisted of 135 Commissioners, but only 68 of them ever sat in judgement (and they were all firm Parliamentarians). The prosecution's case was led by Solicitor General John Cooke. Charles's trial on charges of high treason and 'other high crimes' began on 20 January 1649, but he refused to enter a plea, claiming that no court had jurisdiction over a monarch. He believed that his own authority to rule had been given to him by God and by the traditions and laws of England when he was crowned and anointed, and that the power wielded by those trying him was simply that of a force of arms. Charles insisted that the trial was illegal. When urged to enter a plea, he stated his objection with the words: 'I would know by what power I am called hither, by what lawful authority ... ?' The court, by contrast, proposed an interpretation of the law that legitimised the trial, which was founded on '... the fundamental proposition that the King of England was not a person, but an office whose every occupant was entrusted with a limited power to govern "by and according to the laws of the land and not otherwise".'

Over a period of a week, when Charles was asked to plead three times, he refused. It was then normal practice to take a refusal to plead as *pro confesso*: an admission of guilt, which meant that the prosecution could not call witnesses to its case. However, the trial did hear witnesses but, after only a week of testimony and argument, Charles was declared 'guilty' and sentenced to death. Fifty-nine of the Commissioners signed Charles's death warrant. After the ruling, he was led from St. James's Palace, where he was confined, to the Palace of Whitehall. An execution scaffold had been erected in front of the Banqueting House.

EXECUTION

He was beheaded quickly, only a few days after his 'guilty' verdict. It is said that he wore two shirts to stop the cold weather from making him shiver – he did not want the crowd to think he was shaking from fear. It is an action that signifies a brave, if misguided man. No one would say about him that he went to his death in a craven or shameful manner. He was a king, and would behave like one.

At his execution, he was separated from the people by large ranks of soldiers, and his last speech was heard only by those standing beside him on the scaffold. He declared that he had desired the liberty and freedom of the people as much as any, 'but I must tell you that their liberty and freedom consists in having government .... It is not their having a share in the government; that is nothing appertaining unto them. A subject and a sovereign are clean different things.'

Charles put his head on the block after saying a prayer and signalled the executioner when he was ready; he was then beheaded with one clean stroke. His last words were, 'I shall go from a corruptible to an incorruptible Crown, where no disturbance can be.'

In an unprecedented gesture, Cromwell allowed the King's head to be sewn back onto his body so the family could pay its respects. Charles was buried in private on the night of 7 February 1649, inside the vault of Henry VIII in St George's Chapel, Windsor Castle.

CONCLUSION

Power to govern the country was then assumed by a Council of State, which included Lord Fairfax, then Lord General of the Parliamentary Army, and Oliver Cromwell. The final conflicts between Parliamentary forces and Royalists were decided in the Third English Civil War and Cromwellian conquest of Ireland, whereby all significant military opposition to the Parliament and New Model Army was extinguished. In 1653, Cromwell established The Protectorate and became Lord Protector of England, Scotland and Ireland. Upon his death in 1658, he was briefly succeeded by his son, Richard Cromwell, until 1660, when Charles II resumed the throne.

As Prince of Wales, Charles II had fought with his father in the English Civil War, and was then forced into exile. On his father's execution he had assumed the title of King and had been crowned at Scone in 1651. Leading poorly organised forces into England, however, he had met with defeat at Worcester that same year. He spent the next nine years in impoverished exile until he was summoned back by a Parliament fearing military despotism. In 1662, he married the Portuguese princess, Catherine of Braganza. They had no children, although Charles II sired many illegitimate children. The throne passed to his Catholic brother, James, who became James II of England. When he was eventually forced from the throne, James's daughter Mary and her husband, the Protestant William of Orange, succeeded after the Battle of the Boyne. James fled to the Continent, where his son by his second wife, 'Bonnie' Prince Charlie, became known as the 'Young Pretender' and tried to mount several comebacks, aided by his supporters, the Jacobites. It was never to be: Mary and William's marriage was to prove childless, and the throne passed to Mary's sister, Anne, instead; Anne also provided no heir; her only son died in adolescence. Anne was the last Stuart sovereign. After her death, the throne passed to the House of Hanover.

Chapter 3
Captain William Kidd (1701)

*'For my part, I am the innocentest
Person of them all, only I have been
sworn against by Perjured Persons.'*

William Kidd

It is a superb irony that a man who began his seafaring
career as a catcher of pirates should in the end become
a pirate himself; but such was the fate of William Kidd.
How successful a pirate was he, and did he really leave
buried treasure behind after his death, treasure that has
never been found?

Piracy flourished from the sixteenth century through
to the nineteenth century and even in the twenty-first
century seaborne piracy against large commercial vessels remains a serious problem in some areas of the
world. Kidd is the archetypal pirate from the 'golden
age' of piracy that existed from the 1650s to the 1730s.
Contemporaneous portraits of him show a well-set man
dressed respectably in a wig and cloak. Drawings of
him, after his crimes made him notorious, conform to
the standard image we have of pirates of that era. With
a patch over one eye and a parrot on his shoulder, he
was the prototype for Peter Pan's Captain Hook – the

embodiment of evil. But Kidd was once a respectable sea captain and a married man. What happened to change him?

BACKGROUND

Captain William Kidd was born in the seafaring city of Dundee (not Greenock, as some have claimed) in January 1654, the son of Captain John Kyd, who was later lost at sea, and his wife, Bessie Butchart. When he was old enough, he became a sea captain just like his father. His first ship was called the *Antigua*. During the wars between England and France in the 1690s, he became a privateer (a private person or ship authorised to attack foreign vessels in times of war), helping to defend the American and English trade routes with the West Indies. After those wars, he decided to settle in New York and trade by himself, and in his own ship, along the lucrative coasts of North America. On 16 May 1691, Kidd married Sarah Bradley Cox Oort, an Englishwoman in her early twenties, who had already been twice widowed and was one of the wealthiest women in New York, largely due to her inheritance from her first husband. His advantageous marriage does mean that financial distress could hardly have been a motive for his subsequent years of piracy.

Kidd was always a rebel, always keen to go his own way, and that element of his character may provide something of a clue to his future choice of career. Records show that as early as 1689, when he was a member of a French-English pirate crew that sailed in the Caribbean, Kidd and other members of the crew mutinied, ousted the captain of the ship and sailed to the British colony of Nevis.

The ship was renamed the *Blessed William*, and Kidd became its captain. They became part of a small fleet assembled to defend the colony from the French. The governor did not want to pay the sailors for their defensive services, so Kidd and his men attacked the French island of Mariegalante, destroyed the only town there, and looted the area. It was a shocking incident but one that netted those who participated in it something like £2000, a colossal amount of money in those days. Kidd wasn't content with this, however: some time later, he captured an enemy privateer off the coast of New England and was awarded £150 for his successful privateering in the Caribbean.

It should be noted that none of this was criminal behaviour. As a privateer Kidd would have been authorised with letters of marque to attack foreign shipping during wartime. A 'letter of marque and reprisal' was basically a government licence to attack and capture vessels and bring them before Admiralty courts for condemnation and sale. Cruising for prizes with a letter of marque was considered an honourable calling, combining patriotism and profit, in stark contrast to unlicensed piracy. Privateering was a way for governments to mobilise armed ships and sailors without having to spend public money or commit naval officers. It seems, though, that the lines between the two were often blurred and it would become increasingly hard to tell the difference between privateering and pirating in the coming years.

In 1695, Kidd had distinguished himself enough as a privateer for a certain Colonel Livingston to recommend him as a catcher of pirates to Lord Bellomont, the governor of Massachusetts. A small syndicate was formed to finance the scheme, including Livingston and Kidd who funded one-fifth of the total raised. In May 1696, a ship named the *Adventurer*, with Kidd at its helm, sailed for New York. Once there, Kidd headed for Madagascar, a notorious haunt of pirates. Three years later, however, when he had not returned with any captives, rumours began to circulate that he must have turned pirate himself and in 1698 orders were issued for his capture.

Privateering had clearly been an exciting career for Kidd, but piracy offered him something more. During the sixteenth century, piracy had gained in popularity. Bigger and much faster ships had meant massive colonial expansion and important trade routes. English privateers would attack and rob Spanish frigates, while the pirates of Madagascar represented the interests of the French Crown. Barbary pirates operated on the north coast of Africa and one Ottoman admiral-of-the-fleet, Hayreddin Barbarossa, employed them regularly.

Buccaneers were another kind of pirate hired by governments to fight in the War of the Spanish Succession

(1701–1714). English, Dutch and French buccaneers differed from privateers as they rarely had valid commissions, but unlike pirates they didn't attack ships of all nations, concentrating instead mainly on Spanish merchant ships. Buccaneers were said to have been inspired by the example of sixteenth-century seamen like Francis Drake, who was knighted by Elizabeth I for his daring exploits and near-piratical ways, and their romantic image appealed to writers of the time such as Jonathan Swift and Daniel Defoe.

The golden age of piracy, the one that caught Kidd in its wake, really began in the seventeenth century between wars, when there were fewer legitimate naval positions and many sailors and privateers found themselves without jobs. They chose piracy as a trade, encouraged by a lack of strong government in the Caribbean and other American colonies. Pirates could sail the oceans freely and pillage ships without any fear of punishment. The pirates of the golden age plundered ships mainly in the Caribbean, but the Atlantic coast of America, the West Coast of Africa, the Indian Ocean and the South China Sea were also constantly terrorised. It was the heyday of some of the most famous names among pirates including legends such as Blackbeard and Bartholomew Roberts who plundered many ships and killed countless victims in the early 1700s.

People like Woodes Rogers, the governor of the Bahamas, worked hard to try and suppress piracy, bringing order not just to the Bahamas but to the entire

Caribbean Sea. Many pirates were hanged as a result, some were forced to retire and a few tried their luck on their own in the Atlantic Ocean. However, around 1730 increased military presence and international anti-piracy laws finally put an end to the golden age of piracy.

TRIAL

Kidd had acquired a small hoard of treasure from looting ships that he had captured and on his way to Boston in 1699, ostensibly to clear his name, he buried his ill-gotten gains on Gardiners Island, a small island located between the two peninsulas at the eastern end of Long Island. Kidd duly sailed for Boston and, on arrival, he was arrested on the orders of Bellomont and placed in Stone Prison, where he spent most of his time in solitary confinement under extremely harsh conditions. His wife, Sarah, was also imprisoned.

Eventually, though, he was sent back to England to stand trial for piracy and in April 1701 a drunken Kidd was brought to the House of Commons, and then before the Old Bailey a month later. He had nine associates in all, and they were tried with him: Nicholas Churchill, James Howe, Robert Lamley, William Jenkins, Gabriel Loff, Hugh Parrot, Richard Barlicorn, Abel Owens and Darby Mullins. All of them had been rounded up easily and charged with him – easily because some of them had sadly and erroneously thought that surrendering to the authorities would mean a pardon.

Dr Oxenden was the Admiralty judge who charged the jury, finding 'true bills' against Kidd for murder and piracy and against the others for piracy. Kidd refused to plead and asked for counsel, who at this time were only allowed to argue points of law for the defence. When asked why he refused to plead, Kidd explained that he wanted to put off the trial for as long as possible in order to get his evidence together. His papers had been seized, he claimed, papers including the French passes that showed that the vessels he had captured during his years abroad were in fact his lawful prize.

This claim would later prove crucial to his defence. A wrangle ensued in Court, during which Kidd repeated that he 'wasn't ready', and the Recorder retorted, 'Nor never will, if you can help it.' But he still refused to plead, and so the Court had no choice but to proceed to take the pleas of others. There was more difficulty here as Churchill, the first of the men to come forward, wanted to raise the plea that he came in under 'King's Proclamation', but he was told that he must first plead. So he pleaded 'Not Guilty', as did every single one of the others. Kidd was called on once more to plead, and once again he refused, repeating his protest about his missing papers. He was then told that if he refused to plead at all he faced a penalty of condemnation without trial. Only then did he decide to plead 'Not Guilty' as well.

The charge levelled at Kidd's head was that in October 1697, Kidd had murdered his gunner, William Moore, by striking him on the head with a bucket. The *Adventurer* was cruising off the coast of Malabar when this incident was said to have taken place. About a fortnight before this, the *Adventurer* and her crew had fallen in with a Dutch vessel, the *Loyal Captain*, of which a man called Hoar was the master. There had been some talk of taking her and sharing her bounty among the crew, but she was allowed on her way unharmed, and this decision seems to have caused some bad feeling among Kidd's crew: some of the men wanted to take her, some agreed with the decision to leave her alone.

No doubt this arguing had escalated, for, as Moore was grinding a chisel, Kidd had apparently approached him and questioned him about a safe plan Moore had for taking the Dutch ship. Moore denied he had any plan at all, but Kidd didn't believe him, possibly suspecting an ambush or worse, some kind of mutiny among his men. In the ensuing altercation, Kidd called Moore a 'lousy dog' and Moore, in turn, had reproached Kidd with the words: 'If I am a lousy dog, you have made me so. You have brought me to ruin and many more.'

Kidd took several turns up and down the deck, muttering, 'Have I ruined you, you dog?' and then, seizing a bucket bound with iron hoops, he struck Moore on the right side of the head. A surgeon was then called and he later testified that the gunner was a healthy man who had died of this severe blow to the head the very next day. Kidd's defence was that there had been a mutiny because he would not take the *Loyal Captain*, and Moore was its ringleader.

'So,' testified Kidd at last, 'I took up a bucket and just throwed it at him and said, "You are a rogue to make such a motion".' Unfortunately there were witnesses who did not agree with Kidd's testimony: one of his former crewmen testified that Kidd did not throw the bucket at all, but that he held it by the strap, making the blow that much harder; another denied any evidence of mutinous talk. The Lord Chief Baron summed up. He put Kidd's version to the jury and asked them to consider whether the words alleged to have been spoken by Moore were enough of a provocation to cause Kidd to attack his gunner. Kidd asked the court to call witnesses to his past services, who could testify to his previous good conduct, his bravery and his missions for the Crown, but it was too late. He was found 'guilty' of murder. Some have criticised the trial proceedings for taking the testimony of two of Kidd's former crewmen, who reputedly testified against him in exchange for their own pardons, while others have argued that the judge's summing-up was unfair.

After the 'guilty' verdict, Kidd still had to stand trial for another charge of piracy, along with his nine fellow pirates. They were all charged with unlawful capture of the *Quedagh Merchant* on 30 January 1698.

What had happened during this incident? The story begins when Kidd's ship left New York in July 1696, heading for Madagascar. Instead of capturing pirates as he was charged, however, he set off for the coast of India instead, to look for Indian vessels. His first capture

was a ship captained by an Englishman who was subsequently taken prisoner and hidden in the hold, along
with a Portuguese man. In October, Moore was murdered, and in November they captured a ship from the
Indian port of Surat. She was taken to Madagascar and
set adrift after being plundered.

In January 1698, they came across a large Armenian
ship, the *Quedagh Merchant*, carrying a treasure trove
of gold, silk, spices and other riches, and took her for
themselves. More vessels were captured and plundered
on Kidd's way back to Madagascar, where they arrived
in May 1698. There, the plundered money and goods
were divided separately between the men. This was
shortly before they fell in with a Captain Culliford of
the pirate ship *Resolution*. This had previously been
a merchant ship called the *Mocha Frigate*. Culliford
was a notorious freebooter and, believing Kidd to be
a pirate-catcher, Kidd's arrival with his men filled him
and his band with alarm. They had heard of his commission but not of his dereliction of duty. Their fears were
soon allayed however, once he and Kidd spoke together,
and the two bands of pirates subsequently fraternised.

By this time, the *Adventurer* was rotting and leaky, so
she was destroyed and Kidd transferred to the *Quedagh
Merchant*. Many of his crew left him at this point and
some joined Culliford instead, but the rest of his men
sailed with him for the West Indies.

During his murder trial, Kidd's defence suggested
that in these acts of piracy he was simply the unwilling

49

follower of his own men. His defence against the *Quedagh Merchant* piracy charge was that the ship had had a French pass and was therefore a lawful prize. While it is likely that at least some of the vessels he had captured had provided themselves with French passes (since it was a time of war and news of peace had yet to reach Indian waters), not one of Kidd's six associates denied piracy or said that the documents existed, and no papers were found showing French passes.

Kidd continued to insist that they existed but he couldn't produce them. Did they exist, as he said? Did they go missing? And was the court to blame for their absence? It was subsequently argued in court that even if they had had French passes, the ships should have been brought in for adjudication by a 'court of prize'. Kidd had never tried to do this, choosing instead to unlawfully divide the spoils at Madagascar. His actions there showed just how much he had abandoned the post he had been given.

It was not over yet. A third indictment awaited Kidd: the piratical seizure of an unknown native-owned ship in September 1697. The defences were the same and the jury convicted the same men.

EXECUTION

The sentence for death by piracy was death by hanging and this was pronounced on all those convicted, although it seems that only one of Kidd's fellow pirates was hanged

(Darby Mullins on the same day as Kidd and next to him on the gallows). Kidd had the last word after his sentence was pronounced: 'My Lord, it is a very hard sentence. For my part, I am the innocentest Person of them all, only I have been sworn against by Perjured Persons.' His protest did him no good, alas. On 23 May 1701, he was taken to Execution Dock at Wapping and hanged there in the sight of all the vessels using the Port of London.

It was not a pleasant end. During the execution, the hangman's rope broke and Kidd was only hanged on the second attempt. His body was subsequently left to hang in an iron cage from an iron gibbet over the Thames at Tilbury Point 'as a greater Terrour to all Persons from Committing ye like Crimes for the time to come.'

Conclusion

Those who had initially backed Kidd in the early days, and given him his commissions, were understandably embarrassed by his trial. These are the men who stand accused by some today of depriving him of money and the information that might have provided him with a proper legal defence: in particular, the two sets of French passes that he had kept and which were missing at his trial. In a further twist to Kidd's case, these passes (and others dated 1700) resurfaced in the early twentieth century. They had been misfiled with other government papers in a building in London. For some, these passes call the extent of Kidd's guilt into question, although many biographers are still convinced that he had in fact turned to piracy in his final years on the high seas. And very little would have prevented his conviction for murdering Moore, beyond a more robust argument of self-defence, which would have been hard to argue without Moore having attacked him in the first place.

There is one final, important postscript to Kidd's trial. The belief that he left buried treasure on Gardener's Island contributed to the growth of his reputation after his death. Many songs referred to bars of gold and dollars, and treasure hunts soon began in earnest that were to continue to the present day. On 13 December 2007, it was reported that the wreckage of a pirate ship believed to be the remains of Captain Kidd's *Quedagh Merchant* had been found by divers in shallow waters off the Dominican Republic.

CHAPTER 4
Joseph Knight (1774, 1777–78)

*'The state of slavery is not recognised by the
laws of this kingdom, and is inconsistent
with the principles thereof: That the
regulations in Jamaica, concerning
slaves, do not extend to this kingdom.'*

The case of Joseph Knight tells of an African-born
slave taken to Jamaica and then brought to Scotland
who wanted the freedom to leave the employment of
his master. Knight was aware of a ruling in 1772, at the
end of an English case involving a slave, that slavery was
not recognised by English law and it was his belief that
arriving in Scotland freed him from 'perpetual servitude'
since the laws of Scotland did not support slavery. But
this was not yet the case.

Knight's legal challenge eventually won him his freedom and gave the Court of Session in Edinburgh the
opportunity to declare that slavery was not recognised
under Scottish law.

BACKGROUND

In 1772, the Scottish-born Lord Mansfield as Lord

Chief Justice of England ruled that Charles Stewart, an American visiting England on business, could not take his slave to Jamaica against his will – a ruling that effectively made slavery illegal in England and Wales. It did not result in an end to slavery but it was an important step in the process that ultimately abolished slavery and the slave trade throughout the British Empire.

It was partly due to the impact of the Enlightenment that such a ruling could take place since leading figures in the movement, such as David Hume, were opposed to slavery. This historic 1772 ruling was a great help to the abolitionist movement and of great importance in the case of Joseph Knight, whose case was to conclude with a similar ruling that Scottish law did not recognise slavery.

The case of Joseph Knight highlights not only Scots law with regard to slavery, but also the historical role played by Scots in the Caribbean as plantation owners and as slave-owners both abroad and at home. The main movement of Scots to the Caribbean came in the late eighteenth century. The Act of Union with England was over fifty years old and the Hanoverians were on the throne, although various attempts to dislodge them (by the disparate Jacobite forces still bent on restoring a Stuart king) led to many violent skirmishes. Scots who emigrated to the West Indies, and beyond, were often those who, caught up in such skirmishes, needed to escape retribution and punishment for treason.

One of those was John Wedderburn. His father, Sir

John Wedderburn, had been executed in 1746 for his role in the '45 Jacobite Rebellion – a rebellion that ended in a bloody and ignominious defeat for the Jacobite forces at Culloden. His estates in Perthshire were confiscated as a result of his stand against the Hanoverian George I. Condemned to a life of poverty, John and his brother James fled to the Caribbean intent on making their fortunes abroad as so many did at that time.

There were many government schemes to aid the settlement of Scots in the West Indies and, with Jamaica as the world's biggest exporter of sugar, there was a need for a large slave workforce. The brothers became plantation owners and their sugar plantations prospered over the next twenty-five years. They both amassed great personal wealth on the back of their slaves and their work on the plantations. James also earned a particularly unpleasant reputation as a man who treated his women slaves as prostitutes. He had several children by two slave women, and one of those children, Robert Wedderburn, later came to Scotland looking for his father. (Despite being disowned by his father, Robert Wedderburn remained in England to become a Unitarian, ultra-radical leader, and an anti-slavery advocate.)

After the brothers had made their money, they came back to Scotland in 1769. James moved into a grand new home – Inveresk Lodge near Musselburgh – while John returned to Perthshire anxious to re-establish his family's respectability following his father's humiliation after Culloden. He achieved this, but he is remembered more for his role in a legal battle brought about by the actions of one of his slaves, Joseph Knight.

Knight was born in Africa sometime in the early-to-mid-eighteenth century. He was sold as a slave in Jamaica to John Wedderburn who brought Knight back with him when he and his brother returned to Scotland in 1769, three years before Lord Mansfield's landmark case. When Knight learned that England had outlawed slavery in 1772, he decided to ask John Wedderburn for his freedom unaware that the 1772 ruling on slavery only applied to England and Wales.

Others in Scotland had tried to gain their freedom before him. In 1756, a case brought by a runaway slave reached the Court of Session in Edinburgh. James Montgomery, otherwise known as 'Shanker', was the property of Robert Sheddan of Morrishill in Ayrshire. Montgomery had run away from Sheddan after being forced by him onto a ship bound for Virginia. Montgomery was arrested and held in Edinburgh's notorious Tolbooth Prison. He pursued his claim for freedom at the Court of Session in Edinburgh but died in jail before his case could be heard.

Thirteen years later, in 1769, another slave petitioned for his freedom at the Court of Session. David Spens, otherwise known as 'Black Tom', belonged to Dr David Dalrymple in Methill in Fife. He also sued Dalrymple for wrongful arrest but Dalrymple died during the lawsuit and Spens was later freed.

Then, in 1774, another challenge to the law occurred

as Knight took his battle for freedom to the courts. Both Montgomery and Spens had run away from their owners and been tracked down. Knight was no different and he, too, was tracked down and arrested. But Knight knew the law better than his master supposed. He decided to take on Wedderburn, and brought a case of his own against him.

So, in 1774, before the Justices of the Peace court in Perth, Joseph Knight sought lawfully the freedom to leave the employment of John Wedderburn of Bandean (or Ballendean) in Perthshire. Knight's petition rested on his argument that, although he had been purchased by Wedderburn in Jamaica from a slave trader, the very act of landing in Scotland freed him from perpetual servitude, as slavery was not recognised in Scotland. The Justices of the Peace did not accept his argument. Instead, they found in favour of Wedderburn. But Knight was not finished yet, and he appealed to the Sheriff of Perth.

TRIALS

Knight's appeal trial took place in May 1774 at Perth. The Sheriff of Perth found in his favour, stating that 'the state of slavery is not recognised by the laws of this kingdom, and is inconsistent with the principles thereof: That the regulations in Jamaica, concerning slaves, do not extend to this kingdom; and repelled the defender's claim to a perpetual service.'

In 1777, Wedderburn appealed against this decision

in Knights's favour in Scotland's supreme civil court, the Court of Session in Edinburgh. His main argument was that slavery and perpetual servitude were different states, and that in Scots law, Knight, even though he was not recognised as a slave, was still bound to provide perpetual service in the same manner as an indentured servant or an apprenticed artisan. According to the National Library of Scotland records, in the court memorials:

> 'Each man presented his side of the story and legal arguments concerning the definition of perpetual servitude. Wedderburn blamed Knight's relationship with another servant, and her subsequent pregnancy, as the cause of a falling out between master and servant and Knight's desire to leave his service. Knight's 40-page memorial includes: an account of his life (including his baptism and marriage in Scotland); evidence, partly in French, on the enslavement of Africans by their chiefs as judicial punishments; and descriptions of the miseries of slavery in the colonies.'

As the National Library records it:

> 'Despite Wedderburn's evidence, the Court of Session ruled that "the dominion assumed over this Negro, under the law of Jamaica, being unjust, could not be supported in this country to any extent:

That, therefore, the defender had no right to the
Negro's service for any space of time, nor to send
him out of the country against his consent: That
the Negro was likewise protected, under the Act
1701, c.6. from being sent out of the country against
his consent." The judgements of the Sheriff were
approved of, and the Court remitted the cause
'simpliciter' (that is, it rejected Wedderburn's appeal
without qualification).'

Essentially Knight succeeded in arguing that he should
be allowed to leave domestic service and provide a home
for his wife and child. In doing so he gave the Court
of Session the opportunity to declare that slavery was
not recognised by Scots law and that runaway slaves
(or 'perpetual servants') could be protected by the courts
if they wished to leave domestic service or if attempts
were made to forcibly remove them from Scotland and
return them to slavery in the colonies.

The case was important enough to be given a full
panel of judges including Lord Kames, the important
legal and social historian. James Boswell, in his *Life of
Johnson*, volume 3, page 105, gives an interesting account
of the proceedings:

'A Negro, then called Joseph Knight, a native of
Africa, who, having been brought to Jamaica in the
usual course of the slave trade and purchased by
a Scottish gentleman in that island, had attended

to his master to Scotland, where it was officiously suggested to him that he would be found entitled to his liberty without any limitation. He accordingly brought his action, in the course of which the advocates of both sides did themselves great honour. Mr McLaurin has had the praise of Johnson for his argument in favour of the Negro and Mr McConnachlie distinguished himself on the same side, by his ingenuity and extraordinary research. Mr Cullen, on the part of the master, discovered good information and sound reasoning, in which he was well supported by Mr James Ferguson, remarkable for a manly understanding and knowledge of both books and the world. But I cannot too highly praise the speech which Mr Henry Dundas generously contributed to the cause of the sooty stranger. Mr Dundas's Scottish accent which has been so often in vain obtruded as an objection to his powerful dislikes in Parliament, was no disadvantage to him in his own country … a great majority of the Lords of Session decided for the Negro. But four of their number, the Lord President, Lord Ellioch, Lord Marboddo and Lord Comington, resolutely maintained that lawfulness of a status which has been acknowledged in all ages and countries, and that when freedom flourished, as in Greece and Rome.'

The defence's argument was that 'no man is by nature the property of another'. Since there was no proof that

Knight had given up his natural freedom, he should be set free: freedom was the value set upon life. Lord Kames said 'we sit here to enforce right not to enforce wrong' and the court emphatically rejected Wedderburn's appeal, ruling that:

> 'The dominion assumed over this Negro, under the law of Jamaica, being unjust, could not be supported in this country to any extent: That, therefore, the defender had no right to the Negro's service for any space of time, nor to send him out of the country against his consent: That the Negro was likewise protected under the Act 1701, c.6. from being sent out of the country against his consent.'

The National Archives recorded it thus:

> 'The means by which those who carried this child from his own country got him into their hands, cannot be known; because the law of Jamaica makes no inquiry into that circumstance. But, whether he was ensnared, or bought from his parents, the iniquity is the same. – That a state of slavery has been admitted of in many nations, does not render it less unjust. Child-murder, and other crimes of a deep dye, have been authorised by the laws of different states. Tyranny, and all sorts of oppression, might be vindicated on the same grounds. – Neither can the advantages procured

to this country, by the slavery of the Negroes, be hearkened to, as any argument in this question, as to the justice of it. Oppression and iniquity are not palliated by the gain and advantage acquired to the authors of them. But the expediency of the institution, even for the subjects of Great Britain, is much doubted of by those who are best acquainted with the state of the colonies; and some enlightened men of modern times have thought that sugar and tobacco might be cultivated without the slavery of Negroes.

The dominion, therefore, given by the law of Jamaica over the pursuer, a foreigner there, being unjust, can receive no aid from the laws of this country. The modification proposed of this claim of slavery, makes no difference on the merits of the question. It is plain, that, to give the defender any right over the pursuer, the positive law of Jamaica must always be resorted to; consequently, the question recurs, Whether that law ought to be enforced beyond its territory? But a service for life, without wages, is, in fact, slavery. The law of Scotland would not support a voluntary contract in these terms; and, even where wages are stipulated, such a contract has been voided by the Court; Allan and Mearns *contra* Skene and Burnet, No. 5, p. 9454, *voce* Pactum Illicitum.'

Conclusion

Knight's win in 1778 provided an important contribution to the end of slavery in Scotland and the United Kingdom as a whole. In 1787, the Society for Effecting the Abolition of the Slave Trade was founded and among its founders were five members of an informal group of six Quakers who had pioneered the movement in 1783, when the first petition against the slave trade was presented to Parliament. The Society wrote and published anti-slavery books, pamphlets and posters, held anti-slavery rallies and presented further petitions to the House of Commons.

William Wilberforce, the English politician and philanthropist, was persuaded to lend his support to the movement and he soon became one of the country's leading abolitionists. In 1791, he introduced the first Bill in Parliament to abolish the slave trade and although it was defeated he continued to introduce a motion in favour of abolition almost every year.

It took many years of work by the Society and others but eventually, in 1807, Parliament voted to abolish the international *slave trade*. However, this Act did not outlaw *slavery* which continued to flourish in plantations abroad. People in the UK continued to protest against the practice, and a common way to protest was to refuse to eat sugar – the poet Shelley was famous for sweetening his tea with raisins instead! Slavery at this time has become a part of each nation's history that they prefer to forget. Some of the profits that came from slavery went on great mansions that can still be seen to this day in cities like Glasgow and Bristol.

Slavery was officially abolished in most of the British Empire by the Slavery Abolition Act of 1833 but sadly while slavery is no longer legal anywhere in the world it is still happening in many countries in the twenty-first century. Its modern forms are different but people are still sold like objects and forced to work for little or no pay. Slavery did not end with its abolition in the nineteenth century and today there are many people enslaved throughout the world. Anti-slavery charities and organisations continue to fight to eliminate all forms of modern slavery through education, awareness and activism.

CHAPTER 5
'Deacon' Brodie (1788)

'Is it possible that the King's pardon can restore
purity of heart, rectitude and integrity? Can
a piece of parchment with a seal dangling
at its foot turn wickedness into honesty?
The King has no such prerogative. This is
the prerogative of the King of Kings alone,
exerted only towards repentant sinners.'

From the summing-up by the Dean of Faculty,
Harry Erskine, at Brodie's trial

The name of 'Deacon' Brodie has gone down in the annals
of crime for many reasons, and his trial was also a remarkable one. Why does his case stand out among so many?
Partly it was the level of deception involved: Brodie was
a respectable man among Edinburgh's citizens in the
mid-to-late-eighteenth century. The city was reaching
its apotheosis of culture – its nickname was the 'Athens
of the North' on account of the learning that took place
there. It was the seat of the Scottish Enlightenment, the
place where the greatest philosophers debated, where science was being born and medical experts being trained.
The dark days of superstition and medieval thinking were
over and the light of a new secularism burned brightly.

However, the advent of the New Town on the other side of Princes Street could not banish altogether the dark wynds of the Old Town, and Brodie's trial reminded people unpleasantly of the dirt beneath the Enlightenment's skirts. Nothing was quite as it seemed – respectability was no guarantee of good morals or good behaviour.

Background

The eldest of eleven children, William Brodie was born on 28 September 1741 in Edinburgh. His father was a highly respectable man: a craftsman and an honourable citizen. He was a 'wright' by trade, that is to say, someone who created, built and repaired, in his case, cabinets and other domestic wooden structures. He was also a freeman of the city and a deacon of his trade guild, as well as a member of the city council. William must have been impressed by his father's achievements for he followed him into the same line of business. He, too, became a respectable and highly thought of cabinet-maker and he also engaged in the same kind of civil activity as his father, being active in the community and gaining for himself the reputation of an honourable citizen.

Ironically, however, his carpentry skills may very well have been responsible for the very gallows that hanged him, for while it is hard to be completely sure, it is almost certain that he was indeed executed by a gallows of his own design. And his respectable trade and good reputation among his fellow citizens were belied by his nefarious night-time activities, as his trial would make clear. Gaming and attending cockpits were only two of his many vices. He was a man who liked the good life (and one wonders how much of this came from his father). He would drink well into the night, and he pre-ferred maintaining mistresses to getting married. One mistress, Anne Grant, bore him three children, and another, Jean Watt, bore him two. They would both be important witnesses at his trial.

Brodie's shady activities didn't stop at gaming and whoring. It is unclear exactly when his burglar activi-ties first started, but for many years the good folk of Edinburgh were subjected to a series of inexplicable rob-beries. In 1781 he entered the city council as deacon of a trades guild and in 1782 he became a town councillor. That same year his father died and left him a great deal of money but Brodie soon ran through it all. Financially, he was now in trouble, but he managed to avoid bank-ruptcy and maintained his respectable outer appearance. He continued to socialise with the gentry of Edinburgh and met both Robert Burns and the painter, Sir Henry Raeburn. It is said that Brodie's bizarre double-life even inspired Robert Louis Stevenson, whose father had furniture made by Brodie. It is thought that Stevenson included aspects of Brodie's life and character in his famous story of a split personality, *The Strange Case of Dr. Jekyll and Mr. Hyde*.

As his money began to run out and he could not

earn enough to keep him in the lifestyle to which he had become accustomed, Brodie had to devise ways of taking what he needed from others. It seems that he began by taking wax impressions of the keys to houses in which he was working legitimately as a carpenter. He would then return at night and rob those houses of the items he had identified during the day. It was a dangerous enterprise – only his force of character and his apparent respectability kept him from being a suspect.

He took this activity to a new level when he realised that he could gain access to the houses of even more people without having to use his skills as a carpenter. For as a trusted craftsman, rich individuals and businesses had also come to rely on Brodie's expertise at fitting locks to their new cabinets and to their premises. These clients trusted him implicitly but unbeknownst to them, he was, as before, copying their door keys and robbing them when they were out, or asleep. In 1768, he went further and copied the keys to a bank. He managed to relieve it of £800. He now had the opportunity, the know-how and, it seems, the lack of morality needed by a burglar to get away with his crimes.

His crimes might have gone undetected for a great deal longer were it not for one final case, and one in which he decided not to go it alone, but to team up with others. In July 1786 an English hawker named George Smith came to stay at an inn in the Grassmarket area of Edinburgh. It was a favourite inn of Brodie's and the two men met by chance and fell into conversation.

Brodie apparently proposed to Smith that he join him in a series of burglaries – perhaps he was tired of doing jobs alone, or perhaps he thought he could steal more money if he had an accomplice? Whatever his change in thinking – ambition, greed or arrogance – it was to be his biggest mistake.

Smith had once been a locksmith (no doubt another reason for Brodie asking him to join him in his endeavours) and he agreed to team up with Brodie. In October 1786 they robbed a small grocer's shop together, and later they even stole the silver mace of Edinburgh University.

They were helped in later crimes by two accomplices, Andrew Ainslie and John Brown. The latter was an escaped convict on the run in Scotland, who was going under the name of Humphrey Moore. The four raided a silk merchant's shop together, and a large reward was offered. But to no avail – the authorities were no closer to catching the robbers, who seemed to be one step ahead at every turn.

In March 1786, the four men, emboldened by their recent successes, hatched their most audacious plan yet: to rob the Excise Office in the Canongate. Brodie knew the buildings well because he had often been called in to make repairs. Also a distant relation of his worked there. He knew that the Excise Office was empty after office hours and he knew the layout of the building very well. Brodie and Smith decided they would call at the Excise Office on the pretext of making an enquiry about Brodie's relative. While they were there, Brodie created a diversion so that Smith could take an impression of the key of the outer door to make a duplicate. Ainslie was also keeping watch – he kept an eye on the night watchman to learn his habits and that way he learned that every night from eight till ten o'clock, the office was left without a guard.

The four men met on 4 March to make their final preparations for the robbery the next night. Quite bizarrely, Brodie held a dinner party for some respectable fellow citizens before the robbery that night, presiding over his guests in a white suit. Was this dinner his alibi if anything went wrong? Or was it a kind of celebration in advance? He dined at home until eight o'clock, a whole hour past the time when the four of them were meant to rendezvous. Why did he take so long? Had he become complacent about his abilities?

Whatever the reason, Brodie changed quickly into black clothes, and joined his accomplices. Ainslie was to stay on watch outside the building and, if alarmed by anything, to blow a whistle. Brodie himself was to go inside the building but lurk in the hallway, and keep watch there. Brown and Smith would together force open the doors and the desks. At this point, though, Brown hadn't yet arrived, so Brodie went to look for him. He eventually found him, and Brown and Smith went about their business.

It was a shambolic business from start to finish. From Brodie's late show, to Brown's disappearance, to the actual robbery itself and their final haul, which totalled a miserable £17, the whole enterprise was ill-conceived and badly carried out. The front door crashed shut as they were gathering their haul: unbeknownst to any of them, a young servant-girl had been watching Ainslie. At the crashing of the door, he whistled and fled, but another person had run out of the building already: Brodie himself. He had heard Mr Bonar, the Solicitor of Excise, arriving to fetch a paper he had left behind in his office, and he made a speedy getaway without regard for his partners in crime.

Brodie ran home alone, where he changed out of his dark clothes before proceeding to the house of his mistress, Jean Watt. This would give him an alibi for later on that night, just as the dinner party gave him an alibi for earlier that evening. The next day he met his associates, who were not at all pleased with his absconding and leaving them to it. They shared out what they had taken nevertheless, as the town rang with the news of the robbery at the Excise Office. They clearly thought they had gotten away with their crime.

But it was not to be. Smith and Ainslie were arrested the very next day and taken to the Tolbooth. Brodie went to the Tolbooth to see the criminals for himself, a remarkable and daring play for his own innocence, perhaps, but yet another instance of his own arrogance. He simply didn't believe he would ever be caught.

What kind of man was 'Deacon' Brodie? Two-faced perhaps; of dubious morals certainly. He doesn't appear to have been stupid man and yet, these actions of his, in the light of his conviction, seem extraordinarily stupid. A clever man would surely have kept his distance.

When Brodie learned that he wasn't going to be allowed to see Smith and Ainslie, however, the penny seems to have finally dropped and the realisation hit him that he could be linked with this crime. He had only Smith and Ainslie's honour to rely on, that they wouldn't give him up, and that was scarcely a sure thing. He decided on the Sunday that his best course of action was to flee.

As soon as Smith learned that he had gone, he named Brodie in a confession. Ainslie followed his example, and officials quickly managed to trace Brodie – first to London and then to Amsterdam, after he foolishly entrusted some incriminating letters to fellow travellers. He was seized there and extradited to London. Shortly after this, he was returned to Edinburgh, arriving on 17 July 1788. Smith and Ainslie had tried to escape from prison but failed; Brown had been arrested for murder. All four men were now in prison.

Brown managed to earn a pardon for himself. He couldn't give evidence (since a convicted felon wasn't regarded as a reliable witness) so to render him available to testify against his partners in crime, he was given a pardon for all his own previous crimes. Smith tried confession as a means of escaping the trial but this did not work. Only Ainslie of the three remaining partners in crime was successful in his attempts to escape the law. It meant that following one form of legal wrangling after another, only Brodie and Smith were charged to stand trial, while their companions-in-crime, Brown and Ainslie, were free men.

Trial

The trial began on 27 August 1788. It was incredibly quick by today's standards, lasting only twenty-one hours. Both Smith and Brodie pleaded 'not guilty'. There were five judges: Lord Braxfield, the Lord Justice Clerk, presided and was accompanied by Lord Hailes, Lord Eskgrove, Lord Stonefield and Lord Swinton. A distinguished bar had been retained: the Lord Advocate, the Solicitor-General, Mr Tait and Mr Murray for the prosecution; for the defence, the Dean of Faculty (Harry Erskine), Mr Wight and Mr Hay for Brodie, Mr Clerk and Mr Hamilton for Smith.

A long string of witnesses for Smith entered the witness box first, although Smith's wife was not allowed to appear. Witness number twenty-six was Ainslie himself. The cross examination that took place was to establish the veracity of Brodie's alibi. Then Brown testified, and was closely questioned to the extent that he lost his temper. Mr Clerk, for Smith, focused on the making of the duplicate key, and pronounced Brown's answers highly unsatisfactory. Smith and Brodie's statements were both read out as well as the incriminating letters Brodie had written while crossing to Holland.

Brodie's witnesses then followed. They were called to

prove an alibi and the first was his brother-in-law. He claimed to have been with Brodie until just before eight o'clock on the night of the robbery. Jean Watt followed, after denying she had conducted a secret marriage with Brodie in prison, and she claimed that Brodie had joined her just after eight and stayed with her all night. Her maid also testified to the time, claiming to have heard the bell of the Tron Church. Other witnesses claimed to have seen Brodie leaving Jean Watt's house the next morning.

At one o'clock in the morning, the Lord Advocate began his summing-up speech. Smith's defence, Mr Clerk, stood up to make his case for his client but only succeeded in causing an uproar. 'Gentlemen,' he said, 'I think a great deal of most improper evidence has been received in this case for the Crown.' The judges admonished him and he continued, 'I beg to assail at the outset the evidence of these two corbies, or infernal scoundrels.' He was warned to take care over what he said but continued anyway to say that Brown should never have been received as a witness in any case at all. Bystanders broke into loud applause. Mr Clerk continued, 'Your lordships should not have admitted him, and of that the jury will now judge.' At this the judges protested that he was attacking them, but he answered, 'I am attacking the villain of a witness, who, I tell your lordship, is not worth his weight in hemp.'

The Dean of Faculty then tried to quieten him but he continued to argue against the admission of Brown's testimony, shouting as he left, 'Hang my client if you dare, my lord, without hearing me in his defence.' The court was almost in uproar at this behaviour and the hapless lords were left, unsure what to do. They finally gave in and allowed Mr Clerk back into the courtroom, and let him continue.

The Dean of Faculty had to sum up for Brodie. He also attacked the accomplices, but on safer ground, arguing that though their evidence was admissible, it could not be believed.

> 'Is it possible that a King's pardon can restore purity of heart, rectitude and integrity? Can a piece of parchment with a seal dangling at its foot turn wickedness into honour? The King has no such prerogative. This is the prerogative of the King of Kings alone, exerted only towards repentant sinners.'

It was ridiculous, he argued, that one man's life should weigh on the word of a felon. His main focus, though, was Brodie's alibi. If the jury were to accept his evidence, it would mean that Brodie could not have been present at the crime.

The summing-up asked only one question – who committed the offence? There had been an offence – that was clear. After all, £17 had been stolen. Brodie's alibi rested on the ringing of a bell, but the bell that the maid heard rang at both eight and ten o'clock. Attention was directed to the corroboration of Ainslie and Brown, and ended with an opinion that both prisoners were 'guilty'. It was unlikely, though possible, that Brodie could be innocent, but never Smith. And if Smith was definitely guilty, then where did that leave Brodie?

EXECUTION

The verdict of the jury just five hours later was that both Brodie and Smith were 'guilty'. They received the same sentence – death by hanging. Brodie tried to speak out against the verdict, but he was restrained by his counsel. Smith broke down completely, but Brodie spent most of his time in prison before the day of his execution trying to secure a reprieve. Even at this late stage, he was convinced that his outer demeanour, his appearance of respectability and his previous good standing in the city would save him.

But it was not to be. Not even 'Deacon' Brodie's previous good reputation could save him from death by hanging. On the day of his execution he was calm, maintaining a certain kind of distant professionalism. He asked to examine the drop and tested the rope, which he found to be too short. Forty thousand people subsequently gathered to witness his execution. For a moment, there seemed to be the possibility that he might be revived after the rope that hanged him was still too short for the drop: but it was a faint hope and Brodie could not be revived.

And yet … over the years there have been rumours

that after the execution, Brodie was hastily removed by friends, who had supposedly arranged to try and revive him. It seems unlikely that they succeeded but Brodie was reportedly seen years later, alive and well, in Paris and it is said that when the burial site in the graveyard off Buccleuch Place was opened the coffin was empty.

CHAPTER 6

Thomas Muir (1793)

'Gentlemen of the Jury, if the real cause of
my standing as a pannel at your bar is for
having actively engaged in the cause of a
Parliamentary reform, I plead guilty.'

Thomas Muir

So spoke Thomas Muir of Huntershill at his trial for
sedition in 1793. His own words would condemn him
to exile in Australia, and a hard and short life thereafter.
He advocated political reform of the Parliamentary
system (his great mission) at an extremely unfortunate
time: France was in the middle of its great revolution,
begun in 1789 with the storming of the Bastille. As that
revolution descended into bloody chaos and murder,
politicians on this side of the Channel looked at any
kind of political agitation with ever-greater nervousness.
Anyone suspected of leading Britain into a French-style
revolution was dealt with very harshly.

It was in the original spirit of the revolution (to
improve the lives of ordinary people) that Thomas Muir
began his radical political career. However, as a member
of the band of 'Scottish Martyrs' it would all end in
ignominy and exile for him and for those accused with

him. Muir died a free man but exhausted and weary a mere six years after his sentence was handed down. But he was not forgotten and in 1844, on Edinburgh's Calton Hill, a 90-foot obelisk was erected to him and his fellow martyrs, Thomas Fyshe Palmer, William Skiving, Maurice Margarot and Joseph Gerrald. It would carry Muir's words, 'I have devoted myself to the cause of the people. It is a good cause – it shall ultimately prevail – it shall finally triumph.'

BACKGROUND

Born in Glasgow in 1765, Thomas Muir grew up in a religious, middle-class home, and attended Glasgow Grammar school. By his early teens, he had shown his bookish side, amassing his own library, and he enrolled at a very young age to study divinity at the University of Glasgow. He soon abandoned those studies, however, for the law.

His taste for battling against inequity first appeared during these student days, when he backed his tutor, Professor Anderson, against the law faculty in a minor dispute. When Anderson lost his case, Muir left Glasgow University before the authorities had a chance to expel him. He then enrolled at Edinburgh University to complete his law studies and graduated in 1787.

As a lawyer, Muir preferred to take on difficult cases, especially those involving the poor. His reforming zeal was in perfect tune with the times. Edmund Burke's

Reflections on the Revolution in France was published in 1790, decrying the revolution, while one year later Thomas Paine published his most famous work, *The Rights of Man*, in reply. This book was regarded by the authorities as seditious and Paine had to flee abroad to escape imprisonment; but many were convinced by his words, and few more so than Thomas Muir.

In October 1792, Muir was elected vice-president of the Glasgow Association of the Friends of the Constitution of the People. Heavily influenced by Paine, he had begun to take much more interest in political causes, especially that of the French Revolution. Many Romantics (supporters of a new movement in the art, literature and thinking of Britain in the late eighteenth century) shared his interest – William Wordsworth, the English poet, was a famous advocate of the revolution in its infancy.

William Skiving, one of the 'Scottish Martyrs' (only he and Muir were actually Scottish), helped organised the first Convention of the Society of Friends of the People in December 1792, along with Maurice Margarot and Joseph Gerrald. Muir gave a speech at the December Convention, where he read out an address from the United Irishmen of Dublin:

> 'We greatly rejoice that the spirit of freedom moves over the surface of Scotland; that light seems to break from the chaos of her internal government, and that a country so respectable for her attainments

in science, in arts, and in arms ... now rises to dis-
tinction, not by a calm contented secret wish for a
reform in Parliament, but by openly, actively and
urgently willing it, with the unity and energy of
an embodied nation.'

This speech ensured that by the end of the Convention,
Muir was a marked man. In January 1793, he was arrested for sedition and taken to Edinburgh where he was
granted bail. He travelled south to London where he
planned to tell reformers there of the problems experienced by their Scottish counterparts but he found
that many were in a state of panic over the capture and
imminent guillotining of the French King.

Like many reformers, Muir had begun by whole-
heartedly supporting the French Revolution. However,
his support had turned to horror as 'the Terror' began
and innocent people were guillotined in their thousands. Muir guessed correctly that the reform movement would be severely damaged by the bloody events
taking place in France and in a desperate attempt to
prevent this happening he left London for that country. He hoped, in his eleventh-hour bid, to persuade the
French leaders to spare the life of their King but his
mission was doomed from the outset; he only reached
Paris on the eve of the King's execution, by which time
all hope of intervention was out of the question. Even
if he had arrived earlier, he would have had little effect
on France's revolutionary leaders; the dissolution of the

French monarchy was already well under way. There was now a real fear in Britain that it would follow in France's footsteps down the path of revolution.

As a result of the monarchy's demise, Britain declared war on France and because of what the authorities perceived as an increasing militancy in the Scottish reform movement, Muir's trial was quickly brought forward from April to 11 February 1793. But Muir was still in France, struggling to get home. Informed by letter of the new date for his trial, he immediately drafted a letter of his own to the press, in which he publicly stated his intention to return as soon as passport difficulties would admit. Ever the lawyer, he knew how things could be made to look. But it was to no avail and, in February 1793, he was pronounced a fugitive from justice and an outlaw by Lord Braxfield. In March, with no one to speak in his defence, he was expelled from the Faculty of Advocates and his name struck from the register.

It was not until the end of June that Muir finally obtained a passage from France in an American ship, *The Hope of Boston*, which took him first to New York, then back across the Atlantic to Belfast where the ship docked to pick up cargo. Disembarking there, Muir made his way south to Dublin, where he consulted with the United Irishmen at their headquarters and was sworn in as a fully-fledged member of their Society. On his return to Scotland, he landed at Portpatrick on 24 August 1793 and was almost immediately recognised and placed under arrest. Brought under heavy guard to Edinburgh, he was incarcerated there in the notorious Tolbooth prison to await his trial.

Trial

The accusations against Muir were many: that at the First Convention of the Scottish Friends of the People in Edinburgh on 11 December 1792 he had helped draw up a petition in support of electoral reform to send to the British Parliament. He was also accused of being in contact with the United Irishmen movement and of reading an address by them at this convention 'openly, actively and urgently' willing Parliamentary reform.

His trial opened in Edinburgh on 30 August 1793. The circumstances of this trial, in front of Lord Braxfield and a hand-picked jury that contained militant anti-reformers, is regarded as a classic example of the political abuse of the judicial process. Muir was accused of making 'seditious speeches and harangues', of showing 'disloyalty to the King and established government', and also of 'wickedly and feloniously advising and exhorting persons to purchase and peruse seditious and wicked publications and writings, circulated to produce a spirit of disloyalty and disaffection to the King and government.' He was also charged with circulating Paine's *Rights of Man* and of defending as well as reading the address from the United Irishmen. He was accused of attending meetings in Kirkintilloch, Milton, and Glasgow. He was also accused of advising John Muir Senior on Paine's *Rights of Man*, 'a most wicked and seditious publication'.

Forty witnesses would be called in total. Muir turned down an offer made by Henry Erskine, the Dean of the Faculty of Advocates, to defend him and instead, he conducted his own defence, pleading 'Not Guilty' to the charges. His statement deserves to be read in full:

> 'The Criminal libel is false and injurious: so far from exciting the people to riot and insurrection, it can easily be proved, by a numerous list of witnesses, that upon every occasion, the pannel exhorted them to pursue measures moderate, legal, peaceable and constitutional. The charge of distributing seditious publications and of advising the people to read them, is equally false and calumnious. The pannel admits that on the great national question concerning an equal representation of the People in the House of Commons, he exerted every effort to procure in that House a full, fair and equal representation of the people, and he considered it to be a measure (and still does), the most salutary, for the interests of his Country. But the pannel offers to prove, that as he considered the information of the People to be the Chief thing Requisite to accomplish his great object, he uniformly advised

them to read every publication, upon either side, which the important question of Parliamentary reform had occasioned.'

He argued that if giving people knowledge was a crime, then he was guilty of it, and he asked that no member of the jury who was an Associate of Goldsmiths Hall, to be chosen to sit, as it had vocally opposed Paine's work.

The prosecution called witnesses who claimed to remember Muir's presence at various meetings. Muir objected to every one of them, insisting he didn't know them. He repeated that he expected specific charges, not general ones. He also objected to many witnesses as 'agents of the Crown'.

Witnesses for Muir testified that he 'had never been heard to speak against the King or the House of Lords', that they 'never saw him distribute any books or pamphlets' and that they 'heard him say, no members should be admitted into the societies who were inclined to faction.'

Muir's trial lasted sixteen hours. He admitted he had left the country, but claimed he announced he was going to do so the previous evening. He didn't try to hide the fact from anyone. Indeed, he then appeared subsequently at the Society for the Friends of the People. When he did go to France, it was not for any society. He went purely out of concern that the country was about to be plunged into war.

His return to Scotland, he declared, was so difficult to carry out because of the war, and subject therefore to many delays. There were only two ways home – by Hamburg or by America. He chose the latter course and sailed eventually from New York to Scotland, landing first in Ireland, where he spent nine days.

The proceedings were dominated by the Lord Justice Clerk, Lord Braxfield, of whom Lord Cockburn wrote:

> 'Strong built and dark, with rough eyebrows, powerful eyes, threatening lips, and a low growling voice, he was like a formidable blacksmith. His accent and his dialect were exaggerated Scotch; his language, like his thoughts, short, strong, and conclusive. He was the Jeffreys of Scotland. "Let them bring me prisoners, and I'll find them law", used to be openly stated as his suggestion, when an intended political prosecution was marred by anticipated difficulties.'

Muir's dramatic and strong address to the jury lasted three hours but it fell on deaf ears. He concluded:

> 'I can look danger, and I can look death in the face, for I am shielded by the conscience of my rectitude. I may soon be condemned to languish in the recesses of a dungeon. I may be doomed to ascend the scaffold. Nothing can deprive me of the recollection of the past. Nothing can destroy my peace of mind, arising from the remembrance of having discharged my duty.'

It was powerful stuff, spoken by a man who was anticipating his own martyrdom, and who was ready to embrace it. Lord Braxfield didn't disappoint him in that respect. He dismissed the evidence of Muir's twenty-one witnesses, summing up:

> 'Government in this country is made up of the landed interest, which alone has a right to be represented; as for the rabble, who have nothing but personal property, what hold has the nation of them? What security for the payment of their taxes? They may pack up all their property on their backs, and leave the country in the twinkling of an eye.'

Muir was applauded at the end of his speech, but the jury found him 'guilty' nonetheless. He was sentenced 'to be transported beyond seas to such place as his Majesty, with the advice of his Privy Council, shall appoint, and that for the space of fourteen years from this date ....'

Conclusion

Many prominent politicians and writers, among them the Whig politician, Charles Fox, and the playwright, Richard Brinsley Sheridan, fought to save the 'Scottish Martyrs' from transportation, knowing it meant almost certain death. But it was no use. Muir was taken to the Tolbooth prison and on 14 November put on board the *Royal George*, bound for London. His mother and father presented him with a pocket Bible which bore the inscription, 'To Thomas Muir from his Afflicted Parents'. With three of the other 'Scottish Martyrs', Muir set sail for the six-month-long, perilous journey to Botany Bay – the kind of journey that few survived.

After the Transportation Act of 1718, the numbers of those convicted of the most minor of felonies and subsequently transported to the Colonies increased massively. Between 1718 and 1755, 700 people were transported by the Scottish courts. In 1787, Australia became the main destination for those sentenced to transportation. The first convicts arrived there in Botany Bay in 1788. Between that year and 1840, 80,000 people were transported to Australia while 60,000 were sent to Tasmania between 1803 and 1852. Of these figures, 8000 were Scottish, a relatively small percentage of the total figure. It is thought that Scottish courts were less keen to send their inhabitants across to the other side of the world for good. There was little prospect of anyone ever returning, and indeed, only one of the 'Scottish Martyrs' ever did.

But transportation was not quite the last of Muir, for not only did he survive the long sea journey, but even more miraculously, he also managed to effect an escape of sorts. Two and a half years later, after he had been allowed to purchase a small piece of land for himself in Australia, he managed to stow away on an American ship that eventually took him to France. There, he was gifted a small pension for his support for the revolution, but he had little to contribute to the new France and its new political landscape. Like most convicts sent to Australia, he had suffered great physical damage from which he never really recovered. He died, exhausted and ill, at Chantilly outside Paris in 1799. He had done all he could; at the horrifyingly early age of only thirty-three, he could go on no longer. It would take the Society of Friends almost fifty years to raise the funds for the monument on Calton Hill.

CHAPTER 7
Sir Gregor MacGregor (1826)

*'If this interval, therefore, from the beginning
of December to the end of April, be called
winter, it is certainly the finest winter on
the globe. To valetudinarians and persons
advanced in life, it is the climate of Paradise.'*

Many things about the land of Poyais in South America
sounded like Paradise to people living in Scotland at the
beginning of the nineteenth century. From the climate
described above to the European-influenced capital city,
St. Joseph, to the fertile arable land, perfect for farming,
and to cheap land available to buy – it all sounded like
the perfect place to live and work, a place where there
were opportunities for a better life, away from the grim
skies of Scotland.

And so it was that in 1821, Sir Gregor MacGregor, a
former soldier and a descendant of 'Rob Roy' MacGregor,
thought up a plan to sell off portions of land to the unsuspecting British public. As the self-styled 'Cazique' of
this particular part of South America (a role he claimed
was created for him by the King of the Mosquito Shore
and Nation), he had been charged, he said, by the King
to take over this part of the world and improve it. He

was to refine and reorganise the local government there, enhance the infrastructure, expand the army and so on. Not only were farmers and soldiers needed to tend to the rich soil, but doctors, lawyers, teachers and so on, were also wanted.

To many it sounded too good to be true. And, alas for the fates of those poor souls who took MacGregor at his word, it certainly *was* too good to be true. For this beautiful land of milk and honey, the paradise of Poyais, did not exist. The King himself did exist, but he had merely given a piece of land to MacGregor for his own use, not to sell, and it wasn't anything like the kind of land he had put forward for sale to the public. MacGregor was little more than a conman, albeit a conman on a spectacular scale.

Background

It is certainly true that the Scots of this time, with their harsh history of enforced as well as voluntary emigration during the previous century, were particularly susceptible to such schemes. Just over a hundred years previously, at the end of the seventeenth century, the Darien Scheme (when so many had tragically lost their fortunes and their lives in a disastrous plan to relocate to Panama) had forced the Act of Union upon the country. Later, at the end of the eighteenth century and beginning of the nineteenth century, large tracts of land in the United States were being offered up for sale. Many people took up these offers of cheap land and the chance to be their own master, something that could never happen for them in the 'Old Country'; and many of these offers were perfectly legitimate although they promised a more hazardous life than many buyers could have imagined.

It is a measure of people's ambition and, for some, desperation as well as their gullibility, that so many were willing to believe in MacGregor's offers and his promise of a much better life overseas, but the Poyais scheme really should have rung more alarm bells than it did. It has been called 'the most audacious fraud in history' by writer David Sinclair, who is the best authority on the subject, and that is no understatement. MacGregor used his many contacts from his soldiering past to inveigle loans from rich banker friends who probably should have known better; he concocted fictitious reports about the country of Poyais; he ran advertisements and recruiting offices in Scotland's major cities, as well as publishing pamphlets by overseers who themselves did not exist. He traded on his charm, and on people's snobbery and their willingness to trust a man in uniform who had connections to the Royal household and titled friends. How was he eventually caught, though, and what finally became of him? Did he get away with his fraud?

'Sir' Gregor MacGregor, who claimed descent from Rob Roy MacGregor, was born in 1786 near Loch Katrine in Scotland to a sea captain and a doctor's daughter. Sinclair surmises that as the son of a seafaring man he was probably brought up largely by his mother (and therefore over-indulged and made more of a fuss of than was good for him). His family were also wealthy enough to send their son to a private grammar school.

He appears to have joined the army at the age of sixteen, and been assigned to the 57th Foot Infantry, a rough-and-ready regiment with a fearsome reputation. By 1804 he had risen to the rank of lieutenant, and Sinclair suggests that he met his future wife, the wealthy and well-born Maria Bowater, while he was posted for a time in the Channel Islands. They married a year later. MacGregor liked to dress well and enjoy beautiful surroundings and it has been suggested that he developed a taste for the finer things in life after his marriage.

In 1809, his regiment was sent to Portugal as reinforcements for the Duke of Wellington's army during the Peninsular War. In 1810, he retired from the British army – there is something of a cloud over his leaving – and then he appears to have ended up in the Portuguese army. 'Appears' is a useful verb in connection with MacGregor, as everything connected with him is never quite what it seems. Sinclair likens MacGregor's early career to that of a fantasist, happy to live on his wife's money, and he quotes a colonel who disdains MacGregor's lifestyle:

'... he there assumed the title of Colonel, decorated his heels with gilt spurs and his breast with the badge of a Portuguese order of knighthood ...'

The following year, however, MacGregor's wife died and with her death his steady income vanished (although Sinclair suspects he had already spent all of her money by then). He decided to travel to South America by way of Jamaica, to 'offer his services to the republican movement in Venezuela'. He ended up working for the celebrated General Miranda in Caracas, and displayed enough courage in battle to be promoted to the rank of Brigadier-General. He also met Dona Josefa Antonia Andrea Aristeguieta y Lovera, who was related to Simon Bolivar, the revolutionary. They married in June 1812.

In the general unrest after General Miranda fell to Simon Bolivar, MacGregor and his wife fled to Curaçao then on to New Granada (present-day Colombia). More unrest followed, not all of it without some glory being attached to MacGregor's name. He seems to have been the kind of man who courted danger, or at least liked to be close to it. In 1817 he invaded, and enjoyed a short rule on, Amelia Island, Florida. He had hoped to subdue all of Spanish East Florida but failed (Spain formally ceded Florida to the United States in 1821).

In 1820 MacGregor arrived in London with his wife and their two children. Once there, he began to make the most of the military contacts he had formed during his years abroad by discussing with them, and getting their support for, his scheme in Poyais. He even went so far as to give one of his influential friends an official-looking document entitled 'Proclamation To the Inhabitants of the Territory of Poyais' dated 13 April 1821, and issued by 'Gregor, Cazique of Poyais at his

Head Quarters at the Camp of Rio Seco' and endorsed as 'a true copy of the original' by 'Thomas Strangeways, Aide-de-camp and Captain 1st Native Poyer Regiment'.

Needless to say, Thomas Strangeways didn't exist either. The physical amount of written evidence produced by Sir Gregor is astonishing, and very convincing. In many ways, it is not surprising so many were taken in by him, even his friends and acquaintances. This was at a time when South America, which had been largely closed to British merchants, was suddenly being opened up for trade. He managed to persuade one bank to lend him £200,000 (over a million pounds in today's money) and very soon, he had sold a small fortune's worth of land titles to unsuspecting people, many of them with young children, who wanted to start a new life in the southern hemisphere.

In November 1822, the *Honduras Packet* with some seventy settlers on board sailed from the port of Leith, Edinburgh, bound for Poyais. A month or so later, in the spring of 1823, the settler ship, the *Kennersley Castle*, finally docked off the coast of Poyais, laden with passengers who had been promised land, jobs and 'a heavenly paradise'. But the first of them to step onto the wild, desolate shore could find no trace of civilisation. There were no roads to be seen and no towns. They did meet the members of the first ship to have sailed there, as they emerged from their primitive shelter inshore, and were shocked to discover that in all the time since their arrival they had not been able to find the fabled city of

St. Joseph. Instead there was nothing but dense jungle with a few shelters for houses.

Yet, even at this point, they were reluctant to accept that they had been swindled. Perhaps they just didn't want to believe they had travelled all this way, and with such hope, and at such expense, for nothing. And so they unloaded their ship and tried to make the best of the situation. As Sinclair points out, among the labourers and farmers who had set out for this land of dreams, were many elderly people and professional people, both unused to hard work in uncomfortable conditions. Attempts to build log cabins were unsuccessful. Discontent was directed at the would-be governor of Poyais, Lieutenant-Colonel Hector Hall, but they were wasting their time for he too had been kept in the dark.

The *Honduras Packet* was swept away by a storm and the *Kennersley Castle* returned to the UK. Disease began to affect the settlers, with five adults and two children dying. Eventually a ship did arrive, sent to check up on the condition of the settlement and its people, and it managed to take most of them to nearby Belize. Tragically, forty or so settlers were too ill to make the journey and they were abandoned to their fate, while many of the settlers who made it to Belize succumbed due to the heat and a lack of food during the previous weeks.

About 180 people died on the expedition out to Poyais and back to Belize. Some stayed on there but, according to Sinclair, 'fewer than fifty (of the original 250 or so settlers) ever saw Britain again'. In the meantime, five more ships laden with settlers had left Britain for Poyais. Needless to say, MacGregor himself did not set out with these travellers; he stayed in London.

The return of the few Poyais survivors caused shock and alarm. An immediate investigation into the scheme was launched by the Lord Mayor of London, William Heygate, although it would fail to bring any criminal proceedings against MacGregor. Despite all they had been through, the few survivors who did make it back to London still didn't blame MacGregor. They signed an affidavit testifying to his good character and blamed Hall and 'other agents' instead. They still didn't want to believe that the charismatic Scotsman could have intentionally sent so many people to their deaths in a strange and hostile land in order to make money for himself.

By now, MacGregor had already left for Paris with his family and the last of his money. There, he set up another company and once again managed to extract money from credulous lenders, still as Cazique of the fictitious country of Poyais. Complicated financial matters then ensued, as MacGregor attempted to obtain a legitimate hold on the land that the King of the Mosquito Shore and Nation had originally given him. An arrangement that had since been revoked, after the King found out what MacGregor had done with the land (in terms of the original agreement, MacGregor wasn't entitled to sell any of it). He involved an unwitting Frenchman, Gustavus Hippisley, in his money-making schemes, as well as a Monsieur Lehuby, whom he made Managing Director of his company.

However, in September 1825, Hippisley was arrested with regard to charges of fraud. Lehuby fled to Belgium and a warrant for his extradition was issued. Then, in December, MacGregor himself was found hiding just outside Paris and he too was arrested. Even in prison, however, he continued with his charade, writing his testimony as the Cazique of Poyais, in which he declared he was being persecuted as 'one of the founders of independence in the New World'. The authorities paid no attention.

TRIAL

The trial began on 6 April 1826, and was mostly concerned with the contractual aspects of the various deals and loans that MacGregor had been involved in since his residence in France. It accused both him and Lehuby of conspiring to defraud the public with the Poyais scheme.

The prosecution case did make reference to the earlier scheme MacGregor had set up in London, but that seems to have been of little interest to the French court. It was asserted that the land offers were only for the 'personal profit' of MacGregor and Lehuby (who was still in Belgium). It was conceded very quickly, however, that 'French law did not recognise the validity of such an agreement under the signatures of foreigners with no official status in the country', and the prosecutor admitted 'he had no actual proofs of conspiracy or fraud, and that the Cazique had responded to the investigation with exemplary candour and fair-mindedness' (Sinclair).

As a result of this speedy trial, which could hardly proceed much further without the testimony of Lehuby, the prisoners were ordered to be released. However, before that could happen, Lehuby's extradition suddenly took place and the prisoners were detained again. A date for the new trial was set to begin on 20 May. This was subsequently delayed, and finally it took place on 10 July.

As Sinclair relates, a fanciful portrait of MacGregor's ancestry and his abilities was given in court and according to his counsel he denied all the charges:

> 'He declares upon his honour that no condition other than those appearing in the agreement was ever discussed or demanded. The conditions offered and accepted as the principle of the negotiations consisted solely of the right on the part of the French to preserve the French language and French laws and, in return, the payment of a rent of one franc per acre by each colonist after the third year of cultivation of the land.
>
> He declares upon his honour that he never either sought or received, directly or indirectly, any sum of money in connection with this agreement, and that the only pecuniary clause that was ever agreed concerned the rent payable after three years.
>
> He declares upon his honour that he met

Monsieur Lehuby for the first time on the day of
the signature of the agreement, that is to say the
4 June 1825, and that he has not seen him since.'

In the absence of sufficient hard evidence, MacGregor
was, inevitably but incredibly, acquitted. It was, Sinclair
says, 'the only sentence Gregor MacGregor would ever
serve anywhere, for a fraud the like of which has never
been seen again.' Lehuby was sentenced to 13 months
in prison.

CONCLUSION

MacGregor subsequently left Paris, but he still thought
he could swindle people with the Poyais scheme. He
arrived in London, where he was arrested but not charged
and released a week later. Instead of selling land in
Poyais, he set up a new business under the auspices
of the Poyais connections. Bonds were produced, and
subsequently sold. In 1827 people were getting wise to
the Poyais schemes, and indeed anything connected to
Poyais, but as Sinclair points out:

'Nobody thought to question the legitimacy of
Poyais itself, the background of its ostensible head
of state and the authority by which he could cede
land and raise loans, or the existence of the assets
allegedly to be employed for interest payments
and redemption.'

In 1834, MacGregor returned to Scotland and, according to Sinclair, his last recorded transaction in relation to Poyais, took place in 1837 when he tried to sell some land certificates. His wife died the following year, by which time he was without funds and without a home. He decided to move to Venezuela (without his children, who were by now grown-ups) where he hoped to trade on his past activities and connections and, indeed, he was awarded a general's pension. He died on 4 December 1845 and was buried in the cathedral at Caracas.

CHAPTER 8

William Burke (1828)

*'Your Lordships will, I believe, in vain search
through the real and fabulous histories of crime,
for anything at all approaching to this cold,
hypocritical, calculating and bloody murder ...'*

Lord Meadowbank

Few names conjure up as much fear and dread as those
of Burke and Hare, the double murderers who, in the
early nineteenth century, killed at least 16 people in
Edinburgh in just under a year in order to sell their
bodies to doctors for dissection. Their crimes were particularly cold-blooded but it is possible their notoriety
stemmed partly from the public's suspicion of the new
science of dissection. Edinburgh was at this time enjoy-
ing a reputation as a leading centre for medical research
and advancement, but, for those of a religious or super-
stitious persuasion, its scientific progress could only be
bad for humanity. Burke and Hare's crimes appeared
to bear them out.

Burke's trial was a remarkable trial for many reasons
not least among them the fact that Hare turned king's
evidence and left his former partner to swing.

BACKGROUND

William Burke was an Irishman. He was born in Urney, near Strabane in County Tyrone in the Province of Ulster in 1792. Urney lies on the eastern bank of the River Finn just across from County Donegal. He worked as a labourer and in a variety of other trades before serving in the Donegal Militia as a fifer and drummer. He was discharged after the Battle of Waterloo. Leaving behind a wife and two children, he crossed the sea to Scotland around 1818 to work as a navvy on the Union Canal near Falkirk. It was at this time that he met his common-law wife, Helen McDougal, who had two children from her first marriage. Later he worked as a labourer, weaver, baker and cobbler. The court papers at the time of his trial for murder recorded his profession as 'pedlary'. He was thirty-six years old.

His partner in crime, William Hare, was born at the beginning of the nineteenth century and he also came from the Province of Ulster in Northern Ireland. Like Burke, he emigrated to Scotland to work on the Union Canal. While he was working at the Edinburgh end of the canal, he met and soon married a widow, Mary Laird Logue, who ran a boarding house for down-and-outs in Tanner's Close in the city. He was considered a violent man when he was drunk and was often caught up in fights and bar brawls. Soon after Burke arrived in Edinburgh with Helen McDougal, they found lodgings with a carter called Brogan two closes away from Tanner's Close. Burke and Hare became good friends.

It is thought that Burke and Hare first began their killing spree in 1827 and it continued well into the following year. They had come to their crimes by accident. An elderly man named Dougal had died owing Hare some rent money. They decided to sell his body to Dr Robert Knox, an anatomy lecturer at Edinburgh University's Medical College, and he paid them more than seven pounds. It was a time of huge developments in medicine – particularly in what would come to be called 'neurology'. The eighteenth century had fashioned the term 'nervous disease' and asylums were filled with people suffering a variety of afflictions from mild depression to homicidal mania. Then, in 1811, the French 'father of psychiatry', Philippe Pinel, had broken the chains of those incarcerated in asylums and the new science of 'moral management' began. Men of science were fascinated by what the brain could do, and arguments began about whether the mind and the brain were separate.

Investigation of the brain's full capacity couldn't begin, however, without a proper examination of it. Similarly, a study of the central nervous system required an examination of the body as a whole. Surgeons needed bodies to practise on, but it was illegal to cut up dead bodies. As a result, surgeons often did this on the quiet. If a homeless or lawless person died, nobody was there to ask awkward questions about what was happening to the body afterwards.

The colossal amount of money they had received for Dougal's body – to two Irish labourers, the seven pounds or so they were paid would have equalled at least half a year's wages – gave Burke and Hare the idea of going a step further. They were no longer willing to wait for old people to die of natural causes. Instead, they decided to murder their victims and sell their bodies on for dissection.

They decided to pick on the most vulnerable members of their community. After luring them to Hare (or Burke's) lodgings and plying them with drink, they would either strangle or suffocate them. Then they would take the bodies to Knox, who, both men declared later, never asked them where the bodies came from. Knox's assistant, Patterson, who would fetch the bodies and take them to his master, eventually rose to become one of the most respected men in Scottish medicine, in spite of the role he played in the Burke and Hare murders. Knox, on the other hand, did not escape public opprobrium quite so easily.

How were they caught? Both men had made a living as pedlars in Edinburgh so any change in their appearance or lifestyle was eventually going to be noticed. Soon it was apparent that Burke's wife was much better clothed than usual and her husband suddenly had money to spend. The couple had rented a quiet house in West Port in Edinburgh, but neighbours soon reported hearing brawls and screams from the house.

Sometime between the 7 April and 16 April 1828,

Mary Paterson, or Mitchell, described later in court as 'a person of disorderly life' and who knew Burke, was killed. She was only 21 years old. Before that time, people had gone missing, but no suspicion had fallen on the pair. It was only because Paterson's friend, Janet Brown, who had accompanied her to Hare's house but left before she became too drunk, could testify that her friend had gone into Hare's home and then vanished, that the beginnings of a case could be made.

Between 5 October and 26 October 1828, James Wilson, known locally as 'daft Jamie' was murdered. He was described in court as 'insane from infancy but perfectly harmless'. He put up a struggle, though, as the damage to his face showed later, throwing doubt on any possibility that Knox didn't know that at least some of the cadavers that were brought to him had suffered violent deaths. 'Daft Jamie' was only 18 years old.

A chilling picture of the room in which their final victim was murdered was provided in Court papers:

'... a crazy chair stood by the fireplace, near two broken wooden stools – old shoes and implements for shoemaking lay scattered on the floor – a pot full of boiled potatoes and broken glass, with old rags and straw were near a cupboard, on which were some plates and spoons – the bed exhibited a disgusting spectacle – it is a coarse wooden frame without posts or curtains and was filled with old straw and rags. Among them a man's shirt, stained

with blood in front, and something like a child's
shift, also bloody, were plainly discernible. At the
foot of the bed, between it and the wall, was the
heap of straw under which the woman's body was
concealed. The bed stood so near the wall that the
corpse must have been doubled up, to be hidden
after the murder.'

This, their last murder, was that of Margery or Mary
McGonegal or Duffie or Campbell or Docherty, on
the morning of 31 October. It was alleged that Burke
had seen a beggar woman asking for charity. When he
spoke to her, he found that she was also Irish and had
come over to Edinburgh to look for her lost son. Burke
lured her into his house where she was treated to break-
fast. Burke wasn't able to murder his victim until later
in the evening because of the presence of James and
Ann Gray who were lodging in his house. Eventually
the Grays were persuaded to 'put up' at Hare's lodgings
that evening, because, as Burke maintained, he and Hare
intended holding a Halloween celebration and there was
not enough room for everyone including his new friend
and his close neighbours to attend. Quantities of alcohol
were enjoyed by all, including Mary Docherty, followed
by much singing and dancing before the neighbours
went home; and then Burke sprung 'like a hungry tiger
on his victim' and strangled her. He hid her body under
a bed and covered it with some straw. The Grays were
told the next day that the woman, Mary Docherty, had

been sent on her way after becoming drunk and quar-
relsome the night before, but that evening the Grays
discovered Mary Docherty's body under the straw. On
their way to notify the police, Mrs Hare offered them
£10 for their silence, but they refused. Before the police
arrived at the house Burke and Hare removed the body
and it was eventually found in Knox's dissecting rooms.

TRIAL

Hare turned king's evidence as little actual evidence of
murder had been found at his house. The trial of Burke
and his wife, Helen McDougal, for the murders of Mary
Paterson, Daft Jamie and Mary Docherty, began at 10.15
am on Christmas Eve 1828. Both Burke and McDougal
pled 'not guilty'. Of the three murder charges, the first
charge was against Burke alone; the second and third
were against both Burke and McDougal. Acting for the
Crown, was Sir William Rae, the Lord Advocate, assisted
by Archibald Alison, Robert Dundas and Alexander
Wood; acting for Burke was the Dean of the Faculty
of Advocates, Sir James Moncrieff, assisted by Patrick
Robertson, Duncan McNeill and David Milne; and
for McDougal, Henry Cockburn, Mark Napier, Hugh
Bruce and George Patton.

It was made clear in court that 'it is not necessary
for the prosecutor to prove, in the case of any one
murder, the intent to hand over the bodies for dissection.' Burke's counsel spent a great deal of his time

arguing that it might be prejudicial to his client to have all three murders heard before a jury at the same time, that few could be accused of three murders all at once and not be found 'guilty'. Despite much debate, the trial went ahead and the 55 witnesses began their accounts. Most of them were those involved in the last murder case who had seen Burke talking and walking with Mary Docherty. Several testified that they saw her go into Burke's house looking well and in good health. One witness also claimed that both Burke and McDougal laughed 'very loudly' when the woman did not appear the next day, and it was suggested she might have been murdered.

The enormous public interest in the trial, thanks to an almost universal reaction of hatred and revulsion towards the crimes committed, was such that the police required reinforcements of some 300 police officers.

Burke was described in the following way:

> 'He is a man rather below the middle size, but stoutly made and of a determined though not particularly sinister expression of countenance. The contours of his face, as well as the features, are decidedly Milesian. It is round, with high cheekbones, grey eyes, a good deal sunk in the head, a short snobbish nose, and a round chin, but altogether of a small cast. His hair and whiskers, which are of a light, sandy colour, comported well with the make of the head and the complexion, which is nearly of the

same hue. He was dressed in a shabby blue surtout,
buttoned close to the throat, and had upon the
whole what is called in his country a 'sauf' rather
than ferocious appearance, though there is a hard-
ness about the features, mixed with an expression
in the grey twinkling eyes, far from inviting.'

The newspapers had a field day, as might have been
expected. His crime was noted by the *Caledonian
Mercury* as 'a new species of assassination, or murder
for hire.' As historian Judith Flanders notes, 'public interest in the case was all-consuming.' Burke's confession
of his crimes was reported in various newspapers, with
one newspaper increasing its circulation by 8000 copies.

The trial was swift and lasted a mere two days over
Christmas, in spite of the lengthy deliberations by the
defending counsel. After the witnesses had given their
testimonies as to the health of the three victims, the
vicinities in which they were last seen and so on, a verdict of 'guilty' was almost inevitable.

CONCLUSION

Burke was found 'guilty' but McDougal's result was 'not
proven'. The Hares and McDougal left town as soon
as they could, although Hare was later recognised in
Dumfries and had to be rescued from a hysterical crowd
baying for his blood. Burke was, of course, sentenced
to death. After his hanging, attended by some twenty

thousand people, his body was offered up for dissection and his skeleton is now on display at the University of Edinburgh's Anatomy Museum. One witness to the dissection of Burke's body recorded:

> 'Burke's body was lying stretched out on a table in a large sort of lumber or dissecting room, quite naked. The upper part of the skull had been sawn off and the brain extracted, but in other respects he was untouched, except, indeed, that the hair had all been shaven off his body.' (Flanders).

Burke and Hare quickly became notorious, and were popularised in song and on stage, as Flanders notes. A French dramatist, René-Charles Guilbert de Pixérécourt, wrote a play called *Alice, or The Scottish Gravediggers* and Madame Tussaud put Burke's death mask on display. Interest in Burke and Hare only grew as the years went on. Arthur Conan Doyle wrote a short story, *My Friend the Murderer*, that was inspired by the case, and other writers followed suit. Combined with the increase in newspaper circulation and a bigger reading populace, their crimes fed the new wave of 'true crime fiction', as Flanders calls it. No one can doubt that William Burke will remain in the public memory for as long as notorious murderers are remembered.

CHAPTER 9

Madeleine Smith (1857)

'I have now to discharge perhaps the most painful
public duty that ever fell to my lot … I fear
you will arrive at the conclusion that every link
is so firmly fastened that every loophole is so
completely stopped that there does not remain
the possibility of escape for the unhappy prisoner
from the net that she has woven for herself.'

James Moncrieff, Lord Advocate

So spoke James Moncrieff, Lord Advocate and the chief prosecutor in the sensational Madeleine Smith murder trial. He wasn't to know that the accused would indeed, in some eyes, anyway, 'escape the net' that had brought her to the High Court in Edinburgh in April 1857 on the charge of murdering her lover. It was already a notorious trial, for the strict Victorian society of the time took a disdainful view of young unmarried women who had lovers. There were many, nevertheless, among the Scottish public who couldn't get enough of the scandal and avidly followed the trial through newspaper reports. In the end, it was the verdict of the trial that would ensure it went down in the annals of legal history as one of the most remarkable trials ever. Even today, we cannot be sure who really killed Madeleine Smith's lover, Pierre Emile L'Angelier.

BACKGROUND

Madeleine Smith was born in Glasgow on 29 March 1835, in fairly unremarkable circumstances. Her maternal grandfather, David Hamilton, was a celebrated architect who designed, among other buildings, the Royal Exchange in Queen Street in the centre of Glasgow (now the city's Gallery of Modern Art). Her maternal grandfather, John Smith, was a builder who realised some of Hamilton's designs, while her father, James Smith, was an architect and builder who would go on to design the much-admired MacLellan Galleries in Sauchiehall Street, Glasgow. James and his father-in-law were right at the centre of the city's expansion as Britain's 'second city.' There was plenty of money to be made here at this time and plenty of work for gifted architects as rich merchants sought lavish homes and public places to entertain themselves.

Madeleine herself was the eldest of five children, and for an early part of her childhood, the family lived in a large house on the south side of the city, which was a leafier, greener area than the city centre where her parents had once rented accommodation. They also, like many wealthy middle-class families at the time, enjoyed the use of a holiday home, Rowaleyn, at Rhu, near Helensburgh.

Her upbringing was utterly typical, giving no sign of the scandal that would engulf her years later. Or rather, her upbringing was typical until her father went bankrupt. Smith was eight years old at the time, and while she may not have known exactly what was going on, she would have noticed the change in their fortunes as over the next few years, the family moved several times from one rented apartment in town to another. They still managed to spend most of their time at the house in the country, but during the winter months especially, her father was needed in town as he attempted to rebuild their fortunes.

By the time Smith was twenty years old, the family was living at 7 Blythswood Square, a prestigious address. Things for her father must have been looking up. Her mother liked to socialise among the wealthier Glasgow families, which meant that Smith had some daily household tasks, typical of those carried out by a middle-class eldest daughter, to perform. She might well have dealt with the household staff, overseeing daily menus and so on. Practice for when she ran a home of her own, these tasks were all light work; most of the time, she could shop and meet friends and generally please herself. An excitable young woman with a lot of energy (although that wasn't the impression she was to give in court), she liked walking and appreciated challenges. Perhaps, too, she was simply bored with such an undemanding lifestyle. A young woman in her position would have been raised to make a good marriage and Smith was no doubt encouraged to look for a suitable husband. That, after all, was to be her future.

Early in 1855, Smith met the handsome, debonair Pierre Emile L'Angelier from Jersey, who was twelve years older than she was (there is some evidence to suggest that she had spotted him long before that). He had worked in market gardening most of his life but when he met Smith, he was employed as a clerk. When Smith's parents found out an attachment had been formed, they forbade her from seeing him again – perhaps because of his lowly status, perhaps because of his foreignness. He was definitely not the acceptable husband they would have imagined for their eldest daughter.

L'Angelier simply swept all their objections aside and proposed to Madeleine anyway. She had tried to end their relationship in obeisance to her parents' commands but, perhaps affected by L'Angelier's enthusiasm and flattered by what was probably her first marriage proposal, she accepted him. Over the next two years, they continued to meet in secret and wrote many impassioned letters to one another – Smith destroyed almost all of L'Angelier's correspondence at some point but he kept all of hers. She wrote tender letters to him, often childlike in tone, asking what would please him best and making her love, and her physical desire, for him clear:

'When we are married it will be my constant endeavour to please you and to add to your comfort. I shall try to study you, and when you are a

little out of temper, I shall try and pet you, dearest
– kiss and fondle you.'

Over the two years of their relationship, the lovers
could not of course appear together, and Smith had to
carry on the charade of pretending to be interested in
other suitors. A year after the relationship began, she
was smuggling him into her bedroom, and occasional
worries that she could be pregnant surfaced in her letters to him. This greatly shocked the austere, respectable Victorian society when these letters were read out
later at court. Some of the people who have written
about the case, such as Eleanor Gordeon and Gwyneth
Nair, have argued that as their relationship became
more physical, L'Angelier appeared to become more
controlling. Eventually, Smith approached her parents
again for their approval of the relationship, but once
again, it was withheld. She resolved, after that, to end
the relationship once and for all.

Her resolution didn't last – L'Angelier won her over
and the affair continued. However, there is evidence of
some rows beginning between them over other men
interested in Smith, over making their relationship
public and over getting married. Eventually, by 28 January
1857, after a little cooling-off period between her and
L'Angelier, Smith became engaged to another man,
William Minnoch. And this time her family approved.
She asked L'Angelier for her love letters to him to be
returned; he refused. In fact, he appears to have gone

further, threatening even to show them to her father. If he had done so, she would also certainly have been dropped as a prospective bride by Minnoch. Evidence that she was no virginal bride would not only have ended this engagement, it would possibly have finished Smith's chances of ever making an acceptable marriage. It is not too much to say that L'Angelier had the power to ruin the rest of her life. Or so it must have seemed to her at the time.

On several occasions (21 February, 6 March and 18 March) before L'Angelier's death, Smith purchased small amounts of arsenic from different well-known Glasgow shops. On 23 March, L'Angelier arrived at his rented lodgings in agony. He died of arsenic poisoning the next day. Smith's letters were found in his office desk and handed over to the Procurator Fiscal; but the woman who had written the letters was not to be found at home. She was on a steamer bound for Helensburgh, where she was found by her brother and brought back to Glasgow. On 31 March, a warrant was issued for her arrest.

Trial

Did Madeleine Smith poison her former lover, fearful that he would ruin her new engagement by making public her love letters to him? It was the central question at her trial. An attractive, respectable young woman of only twenty-two, charged with the murder of her secret lover – it was a salacious case, and the crowds gathered like vultures. Because of the immense and sudden popular interest in the case, the trial was moved from Glasgow to Edinburgh and began on 30 June, 1857.

Smith was defended by John Inglis, a prominent Edinburgh advocate from humble origins. She was described by the *Glasgow Courier* as 'elegant without show', and they gave details of her dress, the style of her hair, her height and figure, her age and her facial appearance. She was 'graceful and comely', with 'regular features', 'more than ordinarily prepossessing' and showing 'great intelligence and energy of character'. She was dressed simply yet elegantly in a brown silk dress, with a black silk coat and a small straw bonnet trimmed with white ribbon. She also had lavender-coloured gloves, a white cambric handkerchief and a silver-topped smelling-bottle in her hand (which she never used). She seemed calm and cool and almost impervious to the crowds that had gathered inside the courtroom, as she declared herself 'not guilty' of the crime.

The prosecution, led by Lord Advocate James Moncrieff, called fifty-seven witnesses, including L'Angelier's landlady and Christina Haggart, Smith's maid. They proved easily that Smith had indeed made the three purchases of arsenic, but there was no evidence to suggest she had purchased any before 21 February, when L'Angelier's first attack of stomach illness had occurred.

The evidence of L'Angelier's friend, a Miss Perry, was

crucial. On 17 February, L'Angelier dined with her, and told her that he was seeing Smith on 19 February. There is no evidence that this meeting actually took place, however. On 20 February, he was found 'writhing with pain on the bedroom floor this morning'. He recovered later that day and two days later he managed to eat a substantial meal. The very next day, 23 February, he experienced more bad symptoms in the morning, and these were serious and painful enough to confine him to his lodgings for eight days.

On 2 March, he called again at Miss Perry's 'looking extremely ill' and told her 'he never expected to see her again, he had been so ill.' On 9 March, he visited Miss Perry and remarked, 'I can't think why I was so unwell after getting that coffee and chocolate from her.' By 'her' he meant Smith. He talked of his extreme attachment to Smith and said, 'It is a perfect fascination, my attachment to that girl; if she were to poison me, I would forgive her.' When Perry asked him why she would do such a thing, he replied, 'I don't know that; perhaps she would not be sorry to be rid of me.'

Was L'Angelier poisoning himself and framing Smith for murder? It became part of the defence's argument that he was doing just that. On 18 March, Smith purchased arsenic for the third time. L'Angelier's landlady, Mrs Jenkins, was aroused at 2.30 am on 22 March by a violent ringing of the street bell. She found L'Angelier in the doorway with his arms across his stomach and in great pain. At 5 am she called Dr Steven, the nearest medical man. He did not come, but prescribed laudanum (a narcotic painkiller whose main ingredient was opium) and a mustard plaster. At 7 am she summoned him again. This time he came, and prescribed morphia. At 9 am L'Angelier asked to see Perry. He then appeared to fall into a deep sleep but he had in fact died.

A fellow employee of L'Angelier was called for and he found a letter in the dead man's vest pocket indicating that he had returned to Glasgow from Bridge of Allan to meet a lady. Letters from that same lady were found in his lodgings and in his business desk. It wasn't long before that lady was identified as Madeleine Smith. Smith herself told Minnoch on 31 March that she had 'been in the habit of buying arsenic'. She was arrested later that day.

It was on the fifth day of the trial that Smith's passionate and intimate letters to her lover, shocking to her Victorian audience, were read out in court. Seventy-seven would be read out in total, a fraction of the more than two hundred and fifty she had written to him. The reading of these letters, which showed she was just as responsible as L'Angelier for their affair, did finally appear to disrupt her smooth exterior, but that in itself was no admission of guilt, simply the effect of having one's most private correspondence made public. The sensational court proceedings were of course a gift to the newspapers, whose circulation increased with each day of the trial.

On the sixth day, the prosecution wanted to read out

entries from L'Angelier's diary but this was refused. The defence's argument was that L'Angelier had committed suicide, presumably over the ending of the affair and Smith's engagement to another man. Witnesses testified that he had taken laudanum and that he was easily depressed. Why, however, had Smith bought arsenic? Arsenic had many household uses then but women often used it for their complexions, and in the end, it was this cosmetic use that Smith gave as her reason for buying it.

Moncrieff's summing-up focused on the love letters that revealed signs of Smith's low moral character. The Lord Advocate said of her letters:

> 'The letters between 7 May and the end of the year are written in such a strain that really I do not think I should comment upon. I can say this, that the expression in these letters ... show so entire an overthrow of the moral sense – the sense of moral delicacy and decency – as to create a picture which I do not know ever had its parallel in an inquiry of this kind.'

He asserted L'Angelier's right to believe that Smith was his wife, given the physical nature of the relations between them. L'Angelier was depicted as a hard-working man. The trial, it seems, was as much about good character as anything else. Did it indeed follow that a woman who had had a sexual relationship outside of marriage could be just as capable of murder? The trial said much about the values of late-Victorian middle-class society and this is one of the reasons it still grips us today.

In his final words to the jury, Moncrieff summed up:

> 'If I had thought there were any elements of doubt or of disproof in the case that would have justified me in retiring from the painful task which I have now to discharge, believe me, gentlemen, there is not a man in this court who would have rejoiced more at that result than myself; for of all the persons engaged in this trial, apart from the unfortunate object of it, I believe the task laid upon me is at once the most difficult and the most painful.'

The defence decided to attack L'Angelier, describing him as an 'unknown adventurer' (Gordon and Nair). They concentrated on the letters written by Smith in which she expressed her love for L'Angelier – how could this woman possibly have tried to poison the man she once loved so much? They also argued that the evidence against the accused was largely circumstantial. There was no proof that Smith and L'Angelier had met the night before he died, something which surely had to have happened if Smith had poisoned him? There just wasn't enough evidence to convict her, they argued. And they also emphasised L'Angelier's repeated mention of suicide when it came to 'reverses of love'.

The jury took only thirty minutes to reach their

decision. They had spent a total of nine days in court, listening to all the evidence as well as the address for the prosecution, the speech for the defence and the conclusion of the judge's charge. They found Smith 'not guilty' of possession of arsenic on the occasion of L'Angelier's first bout of illness and, more importantly, found that the charge of murder laid against her was 'not proven' (the division of the jury was 13 to 2). Inside the courtroom 'the verdict was received with wild cheering which officials tried vainly to suppress' and which was soon translated to the streets outside, where huge crowds had gathered. The 'not proven' verdict, while releasing her from prison, did not release her from the stain of suspicion but, clearly, Smith had won the popular vote.

Conclusion

After the verdict, Smith was taken downstairs through a trap door to a room where she changed her clothes, putting on a cloak and a straw bonnet with dark ribbon and a veil. She waited there till just after 4 pm, at which point she returned upstairs and was taken outside to the Court of the Exchequer. There she met her brother who took her to the front of St Giles Church, where they both got into a cab. They left Edinburgh on the 5 pm train to Stepps, from where she travelled on to Rowaleyn.

For many, Smith was exonerated but the result of the trial did draw attention to the 'not proven' verdict.

Unique to Scotland, the 'not proven' verdict signifies that the accused was not found to be innocent but the prosecution were not able to make a strong enough case to bring about a conviction. Many were sympathetic to Smith's situation, perhaps surprisingly so, since most newspapers had depicted L'Angelier as a foreign criminal type, preying on a virtuous local girl.

After the trial, Smith left Scotland for good. She may have lived in Plymouth for a few years before marrying a drawing-master called George Wardle in London in 1861. They had a daughter, Mary, and a son, Thomas Edmund, and lived an unremarkable, middle-class life there, with possibly some connection to a more bohemian, artistic world through Wardle's work. However, by the time she was thirty-six, Smith was heading for the United States on her own. She is thought to have settled in New York, where she reputedly died in 1928.

CHAPTER 10

Jessie McLachlan (1862)

*'I never had any quarrel with Jessie. On
every occasion we were most affectionate
and friendly. I was not pressed for money.
I paid my rent on Saturday 4th July
before I pawned the plate. I paid £4.'*

> Jessie McLachlan, at her trial
> for the murder of Jess McPherson

The brutal murder of a servant woman, Jess McPherson, in July 1862 is also known as 'the Sandyford Mystery' after the location where she was found murdered with forty wounds on her head from a meat cleaver. It was the first Scottish police case in which forensic photography played a role, and the first case handled by the detective branch of the Glasgow Police. It is a 'mystery' because, in spite of one woman being convicted and serving time for the crime, many believe there was a miscarriage of justice and the real perpetrator was never caught. It also has one other very crucial factor that sets it apart – in a highly unusual move, the accused, Jessie McLachlan, lodged a special defence, where she blamed someone else for the killing. For some it was a class-ridden crime, where a working-class woman was 'stitched up' to protect a middle-class gentleman. But what did happen that night in July in one of Glasgow's more salubrious parts of town? And why would anyone want to butcher to death a servant woman?

BACKGROUND

Jessie McLachlan was born in Inverness in 1834. Before she met and married James McLachlan, a seaman, she was a servant in the household of widower John Fleming at 17 Sandyford Place, Glasgow from 1855 to 1857. John Fleming was a wealthy accountant who also had a holiday residence near Dunoon, where he would often go during the summer with his sister and his two daughters. At the time of the murder, however, he and his son, John, were staying at Sandyford Place during the week. At weekends, they joined the rest of the family on the Firth of Clyde . During those times, his elderly father, eighty-seven-year-old James Fleming, commonly referred to as Old Fleming, and a servant woman, Jess McPherson, were left in charge of the premises.

Jessie McLachlan stopped working for John Fleming when she got married. Newspaper reports at McLachlan's trial described her as follows:

> 'She entered the dock with a quick step, but she was very pale, and evidently slightly agitated. She wore a straw bonnet trimmed with white ribbon

interwoven with black lace, a lilac merino gown, and a thick black shawl.'

At the time of the murder in 1862 Jessie McLachlan and her young son were lodging at 182 Broomielaw with a Mrs Campbell. James McLachlan, her husband, was at sea on the Thursday before the murder and did not return for a week. She had been in bad health since the birth of her son, suffering from 'palpitations'. Pictures of her show a respectable-looking woman although she had taken to drinking around this time.

It was a difficult case. The only real suspects for the violent murder of the servant woman were a frail woman in her thirties and an elderly man. Newspapers were to take up opposite sides, some coming out for McLachlan as the guilty party, some suspecting the elder Mr Fleming. It was truly a mystery, and McLachlan's trial did not help clarify what happened that night in July.

By all accounts, this is what took place. At 10 am on the morning of Friday 4 July, John Fleming and his twenty-year-old son went to his office in St Vincent Street. After work, they travelled as usual to Dunoon, to spend the weekend there. When they returned on Monday, they went straight to the office. At 4 pm, Fleming's son went back to Sandyford Place. His grandfather met him with the words, 'She's away, she's cut,' in a reference to Jess McPherson's absence. He claimed not have seen her since the Friday night and that her door was locked. At this point, John Fleming himself arrived.

127

All three of them went to look for her. They made their way to her bedroom in the basement via the kitchen. The bedroom door was locked but they managed to enter by way of a key found in the pantry, and discovered her almost-naked body on the floor. A doctor was immediately called, and he found over forty wounds on McPherson's body, head, face, neck and wrists, as well as a bruise on her back. The police were then called and Fleming repeated to them that he had managed to get into her room by inserting a key in the lock which pushed out another key that was already in place there. The police were unable to find that other key.

In the basement where Jess's room was, the police found bloodstains on the kitchen sink, the kitchen door and the doorpost. The doormat also had blood on it and a trail of blood led from the kitchen to the bedroom, as though the woman had been killed there first then dragged through. They also discovered that some of her best clothes were missing, and that the kitchen and bedroom floors had been washed, as well as the face, neck and chest of the victim. They also found an iron cleaver, which a post-mortem account identified as the likely weapon, and some bloody footprints on the bedroom floor that were later estimated to belong to a woman.

Old Fleming stated that he had been wakened by screams early on the Saturday morning at about 4 am, but he was arrested on 9 July. One sheriff connected with the case found his conduct after the murder 'suspicious'. Why did he not raise the alarm if he heard screams at that time? Why did he do nothing about the servant's disappearance? Why were there bloodstains on his shirts? And why were the floors washed recently?

On the Monday night, John Fleming had also noticed that some silver was missing. A pawnbroker later contacted the police on 9 July concerning a piece of silver plate that he said had been brought to him by a Mary McDonald of St Vincent Street. It became clear that both the name and the address were made up. After some enquiries, the police came to the house of Jessie McLachlan and arrested her and her husband. James McLachlan was released as soon as it was realised he had been in Ireland with his ship at the time of the murder.

His wife declared that she was an intimate friend of Jess McPherson from the time that she also worked at Sandyford Place. She denied being in or near the house that night, and said that she was with a friend, Mrs Fraser, until 11.15 pm. She stayed in bed with her three-year-old son until 7 or 8 am on the Saturday when she went out for coal and was let in by her landlady, Mrs Campbell. She admitted she did pawn the plate that day, claiming that it had been given to her by Old Fleming at 8.15 pm the previous evening. He had asked her to pawn it for him as he was short of money. She claimed that Fleming offered her £5 out of the £6 15s she had got for the plate, but that she only took £4. Fleming then asked her not to tell anybody about the transaction.

She wasn't believed. Her landlady, Mrs Campbell, had already told the police that she had been out of the house the entire night, returning only at 9 am. Even more damning, she returned wearing a different dress from the one she had gone out in the night before. Her husband also gave the police the location of a tin box belonging to his wife that contained Jess McPherson's missing clothes. Jessie McLachlan had sent the box to Ayr, from where her husband had recovered it.

Further questioning exposed that the bloody footprints on the bedroom floor closely matched McLachlan's own foot size. Old Fleming was released and McLachlan arrested for murder and theft. That same day the police found the bloody pieces of a dress in a nearby field. The dress belonged to McLachlan.

TRIAL

Jessie McLachlan's trial was set for 17 September 1862 at the Glasgow Autumn Circuit Court. It has since been felt that Edinburgh would have been a less prejudicial location, such was the excitement the case had raised locally. Newspapers were quickly divided in their loyalties between McLachlan and Old Fleming. They indulged in wild speculations that helped to increase their circulations from 10,000 to as much as 50,000 in some cases. At the trial itself, the Crown was represented by Adam Gifford, Andrew Mure and Andrew Murray. Andrew Rutherford Clark, Robert McLean and Adam Bannatyne were advocates for the accused. According to the *North British Daily Mail*:

'Jail Square was blockaded by an eager and wist-
ful throng, among whom the most extravagant
rumours and diversified speculations in relation
to the case passed freely current. Every door was
besieged by impatient applicants for admission,
and it was only by dint of a good deal of struggle,
conflict and turmoil that officials, jurymen and
witnesses were able to force a passage.'

As she was pleading 'not guilty', Jessie McLachlan
lodged a special defence – she accused the elder Mr
Fleming of committing the murder. Fleming himself then appeared in the dock to be questioned. He
said that at 9.30 pm on the night of the murder, he
went to bed, having spent the evening in the kitchen
with McPherson. At 4 am he heard screams, which he
called 'squeals' during the trial. He attributed them to
McPherson's sister who he maintained had been due
to spend the night there. He says he fell asleep again
till 6 am then rose about 9 am. Usually, McPherson
would have brought him porridge at 8 am, and he
found it surprising that she hadn't. He knocked at her
bedroom door, but there was no answer. He found the
back door locked with the key on the inside and the
front door unlocked with the key inside. He prepared
his own dinner that night and at 7 pm a young man
named Darnley called and asked to see McPherson.
He claimed to have moved some fresh shirts which he
noticed had blood on them onto his chest of drawers.

The next day he met a neighbour on his way to church, and that night Darnley appeared again looking for McPherson. On Monday, he got up at 8 am and at 4 pm his grandson arrived. It is not only strange that he change his original testimony from 'screams' to 'squeals' but also that he noticed blood on his clean shirts and didn't do anything about it. He was questioned closely about the timing of all his actions.

Then it was McLachlan's turn. Her friend, Mrs Fraser, testified that she called at McLachlan's home on the Friday night and found her dressing to go out. McLachlan shared a glass of rum with her then they went out together and parted in Stobcross Street. Mrs Campbell heard them both go out at 10 pm. At 5.30 am on Saturday, she heard McLachlan's little boy crying. She went into McLachlan's room and found that she had still not come home. At 9 am, McLachlan finally returned with a large bundle. She was also wearing a brown merino gown which was different from the dress she had worn to go out in the night before and which Campbell had never seen her wear before.

McLachlan then went out again at 10 am and around noon she bought a tin box from an ironmonger in Argyle Street. She then left her lodgings until Wednesday.

Things looked very bad for Jessie McLachlan. However, Elizabeth Brownlie, a servant who worked next door to the Flemings on Sandyford Place, contradicted many of Old Fleming's statements. She claimed she rang the bell between 2 pm and 3 pm on the Saturday and that

Fleming told her McPherson was out. At 10 am the same day, she claimed to have seen him go out for coals and look around 'to see if any person was looking'. She claimed that McPherson had told her Old Fleming watched everything that she did, and that McPherson had called him 'that auld devil'.

Serious doubt was cast on McLachlan's claim that Old Fleming had asked her to sell the silver plate as he was in need of money when bank officials confirmed that Fleming had £150 and £30 in his accounts with them at the time of the murder. Many witnesses for McLachlan testified that she was always on friendly terms with Jess McPherson. One Mrs Smith claimed that McPherson had again complained about Old Fleming in her hearing, calling him an 'old wretch' and an 'old devil', and there was more: McPherson had said she had something in particular to discuss with her that she couldn't mention in front of Smith's husband. This was just two weeks before the murder. Other former servants of the Fleming household testified that McPherson was 'heartbroken' over Fleming's behaviour. Were these just a servant's complaints about her employer or was there something more sinister behind them?

Gifford summed up for the Crown. There were real problems with prosecuting McLachlan, not the least of which was a lack of motive. Why would a woman bludgeon to death someone she had been on very friendly terms with for years? Had they had a quarrel? Had McPherson caught McLachlan in the act of stealing the silver plate and challenged her? Why had the guilty person only washed some of the floor, leaving noticeable bloody footprints? Gifford tried to convince the jury that there was only one person responsible for the crime and that meant that either Fleming or McLachlan was the murderer.

When Rutherford Clark summed up for the defence, he was 'hampered' by the fact that he had suppressed a statement by McLachlan where she admitted being in the house when the murder took place. He decided not to mention this statement because he didn't believe that the prosecution could find any evidence to support the fact that she had been present at that time. He finished his speech at 9 pm and the next morning Lord Deas entered the courtroom, black cap in hand.

After the trial, Lord Deas's conduct was severely criticised. He had not presented both sides of the case fairly but weighed in heavily against McLachlan. More importantly, said his critics, Lord Deas instructed the jury to find her 'guilty' despite the fact that there simply wasn't enough evidence to convict her of the crime. In particular, when a policeman testified that he had seen two women emerge from Sandyford Place on the Saturday night (neither of whom was McLachlan), he dismissed that evidence as a 'misapprehension'. As to Mrs Smith's suggestion that McPherson had a secret to divulge about her employer, Lord Deas proposed that she simply wanted to tell Mrs Smith that she was planning to emigrate. He gave nothing to back up this extraordinary claim which effectively removed Old Fleming from the equation.

The jury considered for only fifteen minutes. They found McLachlan 'guilty' of both theft and murder. Clark then read out an extraordinary statement from McLachlan, in which she admitted going to visit McPherson on the Friday evening, taking with her a bottle of rum. She shared some rum with McPherson and Old Fleming, who was sitting with them in the kitchen. At 11 pm, he sent McLachlan out for more alcohol, giving her the key for the lane door. The shop was shut when she got there so she returned and in the back lane she saw two women, one of whom she recognised. She let herself in by the lane door and locked it behind her. The back door was closed so she knocked and Old Fleming opened it. McPherson wasn't there, but McLachlan heard someone moaning and when she went into McPherson's bedroom, she found the servant on the floor with a wound across her brow and a great deal of blood. McLachlan asked Old Fleming why he had attacked her, and he said he hadn't meant to hurt her.

She began to bathe McPherson's head as she came round and Old Fleming started to clean up the floor, but in doing so he upset the basin of bloody water over McLachlan's feet. She and Old Fleming then lifted McPherson onto the bed. He promised he would get a doctor for her in the morning. When they were briefly alone, McPherson told McLachlan that Old Fleming had tried 'to take liberties' with her a few weeks before.

She had threatened to tell his son and he had given her money for her silence. When McLachlan went out for the whisky that evening, he had tried to take advantage of her again, so she shut her bedroom door on him. He came back and struck her face with something.

At 3 am McPherson complained of feeling cold, so they took her through to the kitchen and laid her down in front of the fire. She got worse and between 4 and 5 am she asked McLachlan to fetch a doctor. Still wet from bathing McPherson's bloody head and the upturned basin, McClachlan changed into one of McPherson's dresses. Old Fleming, though, wouldn't let her go to fetch a doctor, even when she told him McPherson was clearly dying. She went upstairs to look for a way out but on hearing a noise in the kitchen she ran back to find Fleming standing over McPherson with a meat cleaver. She began screaming but Old Fleming promised not to harm her if she kept quiet – they would both be in the frame for the murder if she told anyone. He told her he would say that the house had been robbed. Only at 8.30 pm did he let her leave the house.

No one knew what would happen after this statement was read out – would Deas defer his sentence so that her claims could be investigated further? He doesn't seem to have given them any credence and dismissed her words, calling them 'a tissue of wicked falsehoods.' *The Herald* was the only newspaper to agree with the sentence on McLachlan. Letters were sent to the Home Secretary and over a thousand subscription sheets with ninety names on each sheet were also submitted. These measures worked in McClachlan's favour and her death sentence by hanging was reprieved. Instead she was sentenced to 'penal servitude for the rest of her life'. It was a strange decision: if she was 'guilty' then she should have hanged; if she was reprieved, then she should have been set free. The 'McLachlan Papers' were then published. They included a further examination of the case which led the august *Law Magazine and Review* to decide that Fleming came out of it all just as guilty as McLachlan. Everyone was confused about what to believe. A correspondent summed up the frustration felt by many when he wrote to the *Morning Journal* 'Heaven forbid that I should enter at any length into the Sandyford murder case!'

CONCLUSION

By this time, it seems that McLachlan herself was on the verge of a nervous breakdown in prison. She gave another different statement to her solicitor about her movements on the night of the murder, saying that she and McPherson had passed out drunk that night and she only came across McPherson's body the next morning. Many think this is a more likely account of the night. Jessie McClachlan's statement was duly published but it received little attention. She remained in prison for fifteen years. On 5 October 1877, she was released. She was forty-four years old. Two years later she emigrated to the United States and on 14 February 1899 she died at Port Huron, Michigan, of heart disease.

Was Jessie McClachlan guilty? Was Old Fleming the real murderer? What really happened at Sandyford Place on that July night? The mystery remains and along with it the rare occurrence of someone accused of murder accusing someone else.

CHAPTER 11

The City of Glasgow Bankers (1878)

*'That this financial disaster, which brought ruin
to so many homes, depriving in many instances
the widow and the orphan of their sole means of
maintenance, was brought about, not by innocent
misfortune, but by the criminal recklessness of men
whose commercial probity, high social standing
and professed religious belief had induced
thousands of their fellow-countrymen to place
implicit trust in their honesty and integrity, only
serves to intensify the interest felt in their trial ...'*

This trial, which may well resonate with some of those involved in today's colossal banking crises, occurred in January 1879. Eight bankers were charged in total, all of them respectable older men living in the most desirous parts of Glasgow and Edinburgh. They were held in high esteem but at the time of their trial, with words like 'speculation', 'gambling', 'reckless' and 'unscrupulous' being bandied about, they were seen in a very different light. Because of their actions, the entire Scottish banking system was brought into disrepute. It was a truly shocking case that ranks, according to one writer, as 'probably the most important trial which has taken place in Scotland'. They 'brought ruin to so many homes', as a result of the 'abuse of confidence reposed in them'.

Background

The City of Glasgow Bank first opened its doors in 1839. It had a few hiccups during the 1850s but was later registered under the Joint Stock Companies Act of 1862. It continued in business until October 1878, by which time it had over a thousand partners and a million pounds' worth of capital. It also had almost half a million in its reserve fund, dividends and profits in hand over one hundred thousand pounds, deposits of over eight million pounds and 'circulation, acceptances etc' of over two million pounds. It also had more branches than any other Scottish bank (133 branches in total). Before its final collapse, rumours had circulated among the banking community that all was not well; the large number of 'acceptances' which the bank had 'floating in the London market' had given an impression of recklessness. Credit was being given at risk and there was some suspicion about the share list. The general public was none the wiser despite more and more rumours circulating just before its close and final collapse.

Other banks stepped forward on 1 October to accept City of Glasgow Bank banknotes in an attempt to stop a public panic. At first, this action was seen as a good thing; it was received with a degree of calm and there was no run on the bank. Some even felt that 'a rotten branch had been cut away' and hoped that 'the good tree of Scottish banking would brave all storms the better for its absence.' However, it was a false hope reflecting the calm before the storm. Although no other banks fell in the wake of the City of Glasgow Bank's demise, the extent of its ruin was yet to be fully realised, and when it was, it was truly shocking. After its crisis in the 1850s and its subsequent recovery, the bank's stock had actually risen and many small investors, widows and retirees had felt it worthy of their attention and investment. There was a real fear growing that these would be the very people destined to lose the most.

When the shareholders' list was viewed more closely after the bank's demise, it became obvious that few of them actually had the capital to help make up any deficiency. The bank's books were placed as quickly as possible in the care of a lawyer, Alexander Bennet McGrigor, and an accountant, William Anderson. On 5 October, they duly advised the bank's directors that their bank could no longer continue to function as a bank and that it would have to end business. It was to be put into liquidation as quickly as possible and a meeting of shareholders was convened for 22 October. Meanwhile, McGrigor and Anderson proceeded to work their way through incredibly complicated financial details before finally submitting their report on 18 October. The full scale of the loss suffered by the bank became clear only then – in excess of six million pounds. When a few copies of their report finally made their way into the public's hands, the calamity became all to apparent:

> 'There was something like consternation among the various crowds who besieged the offices of the various newspapers. Men were taken aghast, and could not realise the astounding facts disclosed. Nothing like it had been anticipated even by the most pessimistic, and groups of haggard and anxious people lounged about the streets until a late hour talking over the dreadful disclosures, while general gloom and an uneasy feeling prevailed.'

It wasn't just a large sum of money that was lost – it was people's livelihoods and even their lives. McGrigor and Anderson's report (which had taken them sixteen days to compile) pulled few punches and offered little to reassure these worried folk. It accused the directors of 'reckless mismanagement' and 'deliberate and long-continued fraud'. The bankers had been caught falsifying accounts, lying about securities, taking on bad debts and making false returns – 'cooking the books' in effect. By these means, they had tried to keep hidden the bank's true bankrupt status.

It was nothing less than a national disgrace. With a truly global reach, this bank had been notable for its extraordinary advancement but it had also invested unwisely and supported bad business concerns in

East India and America, as well as purchasing land in Australia and New Zealand. The bank had lent too much money for poor returns and when the effects of that hit them, their response was to try and cover it up. Honest investors were encouraged to place their money in speculative projects as the losses mounted. As one chronicler of the events says, the case was so bad that it was 'even hoped that it might strengthen the confidence which the country had in its banking system', for surely no other bank could have become as reckless and greedy as this one? It wasn't Scottish banking that was at fault, said the defence lodged against some English critics who felt the Scottish banking system was to blame, it was the fault of this one rotten apple.

When the figures were revealed, it was found that more than a fifth of stockholders held amounts of £100 or less and it was these people with small savings that were wiped out when the bank failed. Half of the bank's stockholders had less than £500 of stock and only eighty-eight held amounts of £2000 or more. Arrest warrants were issued the day after the report came out. Robert Salmond, Lewis Potter, John Innes Wright, William Taylor, R S Stronach, Charles Leresche, John Stewart and Henry Inglis were all arrested and charged with falsehood, fraud and wilful imposition. Ten days later, they were all charged with theft.

TRIAL

John Stewart, the only director without an overdraft with the bank at the time of its closure, was freed on £15,000 bail. After much discussion in court, bail was refused in the case of the other prisoners with the exception of Charles Leresche, who was released and afterwards became a witness for the Crown. All of the others were remanded in custody – had they been allowed their liberty, Lord Young said at the time, 'the public sense of justice would have been most justly shocked.' It was a judgement that did not bode well for their trial. The accused men, the manager and directors, all appeared in court on 28 January 1879 and were each assigned their own counsel.

John Stewart was a wine merchant, born in Glasgow in 1818 and at the time of the trial residing at Moray Place in Edinburgh. Lewis Potter was a seventy-one-year-old retired merchant from Falkirk, who was living at Claremont Terrace in Glasgow. Robert Salmond was seventy-four, from Inveraray, currently living at Rankinston in Ayrshire. He was also a director of several English companies. William Taylor, a merchant, was sixty-six, born in Glasgow and living in Newton Mearns. Henry Inglis was seventy-two, from Edinburgh and still living there at the time of his trial. John Innes Wright was a sixty-eight year-old merchant from Glasgow, living at Queen's Terrace in the city. Robert Summer Stronach came from Lonmay in Aberdeenshire. He was fifty-two and lived at Crown Gardens in Dowanhill in Glasgow.

In court, Alexander McGrigor appeared first to give evidence for the prosecution. He said that at their first meeting, Stronach 'seemed completely overpowered and almost unable to speak', while Leresche appeared 'more to have his wits about him than anyone else in the room'. McGrigor's own firm had acted for the bank and he found the whole matter 'a very painful piece of business'. None of the directors had given him any explanation at the time for the banking crisis.

In the course of his investigations into the bank's accounts, along with the accountant, William Anderson, they found 'facts which appeared to us so peculiar' that he asked the directors to meet with him one by one. He referred again to Stronach, saying that he 'was thoroughly and entirely broken down during this period' and had been confined to bed for several days. None of the directors challenged the final assessment of a loss of just over six million pounds.

He also testified that Stewart hurried past him on 2 October 'in a state of great excitement', saying 'he was a broken-hearted man, and perfectly astounded at the state in which the bank's affairs were found to have been.' Stewart stated that he was 'ignorant of every fact' McGrigor brought before him. McGrigor believed him, viewing him as an honourable man and not the kind to falsify figures. He had known Stewart and liked him, although he did judge him to have 'a peculiarly bad head for figures'.

More witnesses were called who had gone through the various books of the bank. Among other things, they testified to balances being wrong and to money being invested by the bank in its own stock. Far from looking like the hand of an accountant, the work done in these books looked more like the work of 'a man who understood arithmetic' (that is a man who merely knew that 'two and two made four'). And yet there was no doubt that it was the work of account- ant, William Morison, and he himself testified that he had repeated discussions with Potter about the bank's bad debts and that he had also made Stronach aware of the situation.

Morrison was by far the prosecution's most powerful witness, to be recalled repeatedly throughout the trial to testify to alterations made with Potter and Stronach's permission. Transcriptions from the trial itself are hard to follow, such is the depth of the financial mess the men had constructed in order to hide their losses. But, gradually, as the trial progressed, it became clear that sums of money had been altered so that shareholders could not see them. Alterations were made in red ink and black ink. Charles Samuel Leresche, as the bank's secretary, claimed that he was told to confine himself to his own department. He testified that on 23 December 1875, some notes, which ought to have been cancelled, were in fact burned. He claimed not to have known that there was anything wrong with the bank at all, until 'a few days before the suspension'.

Morrison testified to Stewart's increasing panic towards the end. 'He was very much heated,' he declared at one point. The cashier, John Turnbull, also testified for the prosecution. A shareholder with £1000 of stock in the bank, he had known Salmond for a long time. The manager of the Bank of Scotland also testified that they had given assistance to the City of Glasgow Bank as it began to collapse. Others testified to being aware that the bank was 'in deep water'. One William Glen Walker, a merchant and sheep farmer from Melbourne who was also married to Stronach's sister-in-law, gave testimony about the bank's Australian interests. Many witnesses spoke of longstanding friendships or business relationships with the accused men. Family members were also shareholders in the bank.

The investments in Australia and New Zealand were gone into in particular detail, especially as John Hunter, a merchant in Glasgow who had had dealings with the bank, and who owned lands in Australia and shares there, testified that Potter in particular 'kept off details' and left them to others. Hunter also testified that through Robert Stronach he 'was influenced by people of more decided views'. One shareholder in the bank, A F Somerville, testified that he didn't even know the bank had purchased property in Australia and New Zealand.

Did the accused know what they were doing? Should they ever have had the power they did? The evidence presented for the defence was scanty indeed and a fraction of the evidence for the prosecution. It began with

Alexander Moore, a chartered accountant from Glasgow. He testified to knowing Stewart for twelve years and of being employed by him to work on family accounts. He also said Stewart was 'deficient in book-keeping' but a 'highly honourable man'. The suggestion that the accused were honourable and trustworthy men who were simply not very good on details and not great at book-keeping was often made in their defence.

The Lord Advocate gave a lengthy summing-up. He directed the jury thus:

> 'It is my duty to ask you to consider ... whether there was, on the part of any or all of these directors, a knowledge of the state of the bank which came to light so late as October 1878? Their own books show that they had looked into the matter, that they had suspicions. If they really and truly knew that things were wrong, they were not entitled to shut their eyes and not look ...'

He made it clear that there was a 'distinct connection' between the 'state of the bank' and the 'misrepresentations or falsifications' on the balance sheets. He claimed that a 'guilty' verdict was enough even if an individual did not personally sign the wrong sheets or pen the wrong figures.

'It is enough if he knew, and was aware that the balance sheet was not a true, but a false balance sheet.'

There then followed individual addresses on behalf

of the accused, and the Lord Justice Clerk's charge. He made clear his feelings about the case.

> 'I have never, since I had a seat on the bench, experienced so much feeling of pain, of regret – I had almost said of mortification. The circumstances that we have been enquiring into have a large significance outside these walls ...'

He also made it clear that some members of the accused could not be fully implicated, like Salmond, who 'was not there. He not only could not consult, he could not be consulted.' In summing up, he argued that:

> 'There is nothing in the conduct of the prisoners at the bar to indicate that they were making ready to quit a falling house, or that they were making preparations for a catastrophe that they thought was at hand.'

Would the jury accept that? They retired at 3.50 pm and returned to court at 5.45 pm. The jury foreman announced that they found Potter and Stronach 'guilty' of falsifying balance sheets; then Stewart, Salmond, Taylor, Inglis and Innes Wright were also 'guilty' of the lesser charges of not falsifying the balance sheets, but of using them and publishing them, knowing them to be false. All were found 'not guilty' of the far more serious charges of embezzlement and theft. Potter and

Stronach were sentenced to eighteen months in prison, and the others to eight months in prison.

CONCLUSION

It was a harsh sentence, given the advanced ages of most of the accused. More so because the shame of going to jail for these very middle-class, respectable figures, who had previously been pillars of their community, was probably greater. They had been found 'not guilty' of criminal intent but 'guilty' of foolishness and incompetence.

The scandal served as a warning to those banks who sought to grow too fast, and for many years afterwards banks did take greater care over their investments and investors themselves were more wary with their money. Sadly, those who had lost out could not recover what they had lost and many suffered great hardship. It was a sorry end to a financial century that had put Scotland, and Scottish banks, on the map.

CHAPTER 12
Oscar Slater (1909)

'My Lord, what shall I say? . . . I know nothing about the affair, absolutely nothing. I never heard the name. I know nothing about the affair. I do not know how I could be connected with the affair. I know nothing about it. I came from America on my own account. I can say no more.'

The above statement was made by Oscar Slater on 5 May 1909 just before he was sentenced to death by hanging. Before the death sentence could be carried out, it was commuted to life imprisonment thanks to a petition organised by his lawyers and signed by 20,000 people. However, it would be nineteen years before an appeal court decided that he was the victim of a miscarriage of justice.

The contents of a book published in 1927, *The Truth About Oscar Slater* by William Park, led the Solicitor General for Scotland to conclude that it was no longer proven that Slater was guilty and he was released from prison in November 1927 but on licence and without a pardon. An Act was passed that same year to extend the jurisdiction of the recently established Scottish Court of Criminal Appeal to convictions before the original shut-off date of 1926. And so it came about that Oscar Slater's conviction was finally quashed in an appeal hearing in 1928, on the grounds that during his trial in 1909 the judge had not directed the jury about the irrelevance of Slater's previous character. Slater received £6,000 (a lot of money in those days) in compensation for the years he spent in jail but he died without a pardon. The victim of a gross miscarriage of justice who had always protested his innocence, Oscar Slater died in Ayr in 1948.

BACKGROUND

There are two victims in this murder story. The first was the victim of a terrible crime. The second was the victim of gross injustice, brought about by a lethal cocktail of over-zealous policing, a disregard for sound investigative procedure and undoubtedly social, religious and racial prejudice.

Oscar Slater was born in Germany in 1872, the son of a baker and his wife. The family were Jewish. Oscar found various kinds of gainful employment as he grew towards adulthood, but when the time came for him to serve his duty in the armed forces, he decided that conscription was not for him and he left Germany before he was sent his papers. He entered the world of gambling in London after he got a job working for a bookie and was soon wheeling and dealing in his own right, organising gambling circles and buying and selling the odd piece of jewellery. He moved to Glasgow, where he met and married a Scots girl. The marriage was a mistake: his wife drank heavily and became such a torment that Oscar left her. Unfortunately, the woman proved to be more tenacious than Oscar had anticipated. Whenever he tried to shake her off, she tracked him down. He was forced to adopt false names in order to put her off the scent.

Oscar eventually moved back to London, where he became attached to Madame Andrée Junio Antoine, a working woman who entertained her other 'gentlemen clients' when Oscar was out conducting his own business. The pair travelled to the United States together – Oscar had visited the country a few times before – and spent a successful year helping to run a gambling club in New York. They returned to Britain in 1908, first to London and then to Glasgow. Oscar's alias was now Adolf Anderson. Oscar and his mistress went back to their former patterns of work quite happily. Oscar was generally out wheeling and dealing all day while Madame Antoine received her clients. In the evenings, Oscar usually returned home for dinner, which the couple ate together.

Oscar Slater was hardly a criminal. He was an entrepreneur, a speculator whose dealings might not have been entirely legitimate, but he was not a hard man, nor a thief. There can be little doubt that he did not deserve what lay in store for him in 1908 after his return to Glasgow.

Marion Gilchrist was a spinster. She lived in a flat on the first floor of a tenement building in West Princes Street, Glasgow. She did not live alone: she had a live-in maid, named Nellie Lambie. Miss Gilchrist was comfortably off and had a considerable amount of valuable jewellery hidden in various secret places around the flat. She was very much aware that a woman in her position was a likely prey to thieves. She kept her front door firmly locked at all times, whether she was in or out of the flat. Three locks in total were used to secure the door. Two of the locks were used at all times, the third was only locked when Miss Gilchrist went to bed at night. Downstairs, the close door that led on to the street was usually kept locked as well, for added security. Any likely thief would certainly have his work cut out for him if he wanted to break into the home of Marion Gilchrist.

In the flat immediately below Miss Gilchrist lived the Adams family. Their front door opened onto the street, next to the door for the stair, or close, where Marion Gilchrist's flat was. The Adams family consisted of Mrs Adams and her son Arthur and his two sisters.

On 21 December 1908, Arthur Adams was in the dining room of his flat with his sisters, making preparations for Christmas, when they heard some strange noises coming from the flat above. This was unusual; one of the benefits of having an elderly lady as an upstairs neighbour was that there were no problems with noise from above. The noises consisted of a loud thump, followed by three knocks. The Adams family knew Miss Gilchrist and were aware that she was nervous; she had even elicited from them a promise that, should they hear her knocking on the floor, they were to take it as a signal from her that something was wrong and come to her aid. Arthur Adams was sufficiently concerned when he heard the thumps from upstairs that night to stop what he was doing and go and investigate.

The first thing that Adams noticed was the door of the close. It was unlocked. This was certainly unusual. Adams climbed the stairs to the first floor and rang Miss Gilchrist's front doorbell. When he peered through the glass in the front door he could see that a light was on in the hallway. It looked as if someone was in, so when he got no reply the first time, he rang the bell once again, this time with considerably more force. He could hear sounds of activity coming from the flat now: it sounded like someone chopping sticks for the fire. Deciding that the noise was probably just that – Nellie Lambie chopping kindling for her mistress's living-room fire, too absorbed in her task to hear the doorbell – Arthur went back downstairs and returned to his own flat.

His sisters, however, were quite insistent that something was very much wrong in the flat upstairs; they had never heard noises like that before. They sent Arthur back to try the doorbell one more time. He went back up to Miss Gilchrist's front door, rang the bell very loudly and waited. Just then, there were footsteps on the stairs and Nellie Lambie, Miss Gilchrist's maid, arrived on the landing behind him. She had been out on an errand for her mistress. Arthur, now aware that the noises that he had heard through the door a moment or two ago could not have been the sounds of Nellie chopping firewood, told her of his concerns. Nellie dismissed them as nothing. The pulley that was used for drying clothes in the kitchen was making a dreadful noise, she said. It needed oiling. It was probably the pulley that the Adams family had heard. But the noises had come from Miss Gilchrist's dining room, which was directly above the Adams' dining room. They had not come from the kitchen. Arthur Adams still felt that he ought to linger long enough to ensure that all was well with Miss Gilchrist.

Nellie Lambie unlocked the front door and the two of them went into the hall. Nellie headed straight for the kitchen, which was situated on the left-hand side of the hall, but just as she did so, a man appeared from another room – a bedroom – on the right-hand side. He had the appearance of quite a respectable gentleman and, strangely, Nellie Lambie was apparently unperturbed by his presence in the flat. If she was surprised to find him there, she certainly did not show it. To Arthur Adams, it seemed as if she recognised him. The man came towards Arthur Adams, paused as if to say something, then suddenly brushed past him and headed at full speed for the stairs. Nellie, meanwhile, went into the kitchen to have a look at the pulley. She came out again to say that everything was all right, but Arthur Adams had other concerns. Where was Miss Gilchrist? Nellie then went into the dining room to look for her mistress. She screamed at what she saw in there. Arthur Adams followed her in. He too, gasped at what he saw. Miss Gilchrist lay in a pool of blood in front of the dining room fire. A rug had been hastily flung over her head.

Arthur Adams at once tried to give chase to the man who had met them when they arrived in the flat. He left Nellie to summon help and ran downstairs and out into the street. When he got outside, he ran some distance down West Princes Street, but saw no one in the darkness. He ran back in the other direction and peered along the street as far as he could see. All that he saw were some figures far in the distance – too far for him to catch up with. He went back up to Miss Gilchrist's flat. By this time a policeman had arrived. They carefully uncovered Miss Gilchrist and found that she was still breathing, although she was obviously close to death. Arthur ran for the doctor – Dr Adams (no relation), who lived close by – but by the time the doctor arrived in the flat to examine Miss Gilchrist, she was dead. A chair lay by her side, covered in bloodstains. This, the doctor declared, had in all likelihood been the murder weapon.

The policeman called for the detective squad, and they arrived soon afterwards to search the flat for evidence and question the witnesses. Naturally, they were interested in the stranger who had been in the flat when Nellie had let Arthur Adams in. Arthur Adams had not been in a position to see the man very clearly, for he had not had his spectacles on at the time, but he told the police what he knew. The man was quite young – probably in his late twenties or early thirties. He was slim, dark and clean-shaven. He was wearing a light-coloured overcoat and a cloth cap, which was darker in colour. He was about five feet nine inches tall.

Nellie told the police that she had hardly seen the man. She also told them that she had been out of the flat for no more than ten minutes or so. She had only stepped out to get a paper for Miss Gilchrist. This meant that if the stranger had not been in the flat before she left – and it appeared that this was the case – he had not had much time in which to act.

The search of the flat revealed the following.

A gas lamp had been lit in a spare bedroom in Nellie Lambie's absence. Beneath the lamp was a table on which the police found a box of matches that were not the kind that were used in the flat. The table also had on it a toilet dish with some jewellery in it and a wooden box that had contained some papers. There was also a gold pocket watch and chain. The wooden box had been forced open and its contents lay scattered on the floor beneath the table. Strangely, the jewellery had, for the most part, been left well alone. The only thing that was missing, according to Nellie Lambie, was a brooch. The brooch was quite distinctive: crescent-shaped and decorated with diamonds.

Perhaps the murderer was prevented from taking any-thing else by the arrival of Nellie Lambie and Arthur

Adams, but the jewellery had been quite accessible on the table. Could he not have grabbed a handful of trinkets, or at least the watch and chain, before he made his getaway?

There was no sign of a forced entry to the flat. Miss Gilchrist had been very wary of strangers. It was most unlikely that she would have let anyone into her flat, especially as she was alone, unless she knew him. The police, therefore, concentrated their questioning on Nellie Lambie. Could the killer have been a friend of Miss Gilchrist or a friend of Nellie Lambie?

It was at this point that the case began to go wrong. One promising young detective, John Trench, was sure that Nellie Lambie had known the man who had appeared in the hallway that night. He was someone with whom both she and Miss Gilchrist were familiar. This crucial fact was later to be ignored by the officers in charge of the investigation. The fact that she had hardly seen him was given greater weight instead, as the investigation moved on in the coming days and began to centre on a man called Oscar Slater.

A second description, of a man who was said to have been seen running from the entrance to Miss Gilchrist's close, was given to the police. It did not quite match the description given by the myopic Arthur Adams. Police published both descriptions in case there was more than one man involved in the killing, but the details that differed may not have been as crucial as the police thought. The girl who gave the second description, Mary

159

Barrowman, provided a little more detail than Adams had done. She described the stranger as tall, while Adams had said that he was about five feet nine inches in height. We do not know how tall Mary Barrowman was, but she was only fourteen years old. She was probably not yet fully grown. Five feet nine inches might have seemed quite tall to a young girl of smaller stature. Mary described the stranger's overcoat as a light fawn waterproof. Adams thought it was light grey. The two colours are not hugely dissimilar, and we should remember that Adams saw the man inside while Mary Barrowman claimed to have seen him outside in the darkened street. The light would be different, as would one's perception of colour.

On Christmas Day, a man who had read of the murder in the papers and had seen both descriptions of the man and wanted to help the police with their inquiries, came forward with some information. The man was a member of a club in India Street, where a man called Oscar was also a member. Oscar had been trying to find a buyer amongst the other club members for a pawn ticket that he had. The ticket was for a crescent-shaped diamond brooch. He knew where Oscar lived – 69 St George's Road.

Oscar Slater, a German Jew, seemed like a very credible suspect to the police. Their investigations revealed that he was a gambler – hardly a respectable profession and one likely to lead to financial difficulties. Slater was also known to buy and sell jewellery. The transactions he made were not quite the same as those that were made in high street jewellers' shops. They were much more private. Perhaps they were a little shady. The police discovered that Slater lived with a woman known as Madame Andrée Junio Antoine, who was not exactly a model of respectability herself. Slater also used aliases; the name at the door of his house was that of A. Anderson, dentist.

It was all looking quite promising as the police made their way to 69 St George's Road to pay a visit to Oscar Slater. When they got to the house, they found that Slater and his mistress had both left. Slater's maid told them that they had gone on Christmas Day, headed for America. A shady lifestyle, a pawn ticket, a sudden departure. Oscar's prospects were looking bleaker and bleaker.

Then the police managed to trace the brooch that Oscar Slater had pawned. It was decorated with diamonds, it was crescent-shaped, but there the similarity ended. It was most definitely not the brooch that had been taken from Miss Gilchrist's house, and Oscar Slater had pawned it long before Miss Gilchrist's death.

By rights, the police ought to have stopped pursuing Oscar Slater right there and then. Apart from the chance that the brooch might have been Miss Gilchrist's, they had nothing whatsoever to establish a link between Slater and the killing. They had no real reason to suspect him any more. Oscar Slater might have been a bit of a dodgy character, but he was not a known thief, nor did he have a reputation as a violent man. There were hundreds of other dodgy characters in Glasgow, just like him. Why should Oscar Slater be the one who had killed Miss Gilchrist?

The police would not let go. Slater had left for America quite suddenly. He was running from something, they decided; in all probability, he was running from a murder charge.

Oscar and his mistress had sailed on the Lusitania to New York. When it docked in early January, police met Slater and Madame Junio Antoine as they disembarked. Both were arrested and incarcerated. A search of their luggage revealed that Oscar Slater was in possession of a light-coloured raincoat, which was stained – could it be blood from the murder? There was also a small tool set in the luggage, including a small hammer. This, the police decided, was the murder weapon. They were forgetting (or choosing to overlook) the bloodstained chair that had been found beside Miss Gilchrist's body.

Oscar Slater had not left suddenly for America in fact. He had spent some three weeks in preparation for his travels, making arrangements with a friend who lived in the United States for his journey to San Francisco and finding another tenant to take up the lease on his flat. He did bring the date of travel forward by some days when he found out that his troublesome wife was yet again on his trail, but when it came to packing up and leaving on Christmas night, his preparations were unhurried and careful and his luggage beautifully organised – hardly the behaviour of a man on the run for murder.

Meanwhile, back in Britain, Oscar Slater's picture appeared in the papers. A reward had already been offered for information that might lead to the conviction of Miss Gilchrist's murderer – £200, quite a tidy sum. After Slater's picture appeared in the papers, there were suddenly plenty of people who felt quite confident that they could recognise this man. Oscar Slater, according to the willing witnesses who came forward, had been seen near Miss Gilchrist's flat before, after and on the day of her murder.

Slater had to be extradited from the United States before any further action could be taken against him in Scotland. To this end, arrangements were made to pay for the passage of Mary Barrowman, Nellie Lambie and Arthur Adams to New York. Further repeated questioning sessions by police had been quite skilful and by now the descriptions of the man that Nellie Lambie and Mary Barrowman had seen were almost identical. These two 'independent' witnesses were, strangely, given a cabin to share on the voyage. When the three witnesses were taken to the identification parade, it was quite clear which man of the three before them they were supposed to pick. He was handcuffed to another man, who was far too tall to be a likely suspect. The other man, free of bonds, could not be the one the police were holding in custody. Whatever they might have thought, it was obvious to the three witnesses that they were supposed to pick out Oscar Slater. So they did, albeit with some hesitation, for Slater was neither of slim build nor clean-shaven. He was short and broad and had a moustache. Nor was he aged between twenty-five and thirty. He was thirty-seven years old and could not have passed for a younger man. The American authorities were not happy with the identification, and the lawyer who was representing Slater urged him to continue to fight against the extradition.

But Slater felt he had nothing to fear. If he went back to Scotland, he could clear his name without difficulty. He ought to have been right. He had a strong alibi for 21 December, the night of the murder. (At this point, however, he was more concerned about his alibi for 22 December, the night after the murder – for so little did Oscar Slater know of the crime of which he was being accused that he thought that the murder had taken place on the 22nd.)

If all had been fair at his subsequent trial, Slater's innocence could have been proved beyond reasonable doubt. His alibi for the night of 21 December, however, was never brought up in court. All was not fair. Moreover, there were, unbeknown to him, all those willing witnesses waiting for him back in Scotland; witnesses whose eyes must have been gleaming at the thought of a £200 reward.

Oscar Slater sailed back to Britain under escort, ready to prove his innocence, sadly unprepared for his assumed

guilt. Before he left for Scotland, at this point still believing that Marion Gilchrist had been killed on the night
of 22 December, he wrote to a friend back in Scotland
asking for support and stressing that he could find five
men to support his alibi for that night.

If Oscar Slater had committed the murder, then why
was he putting all his efforts into proving his where-
abouts on the wrong night? The day one commits murder
is surely not one so easily forgotten. This fact, like so
many others crucial to the case, was to be ignored. Back
in Glasgow another identification parade awaited.

This time Oscar was placed in a line with some police-
men in plain clothes and some railway officials. Bear in
mind that Oscar was a foreigner – and he looked foreign.
The men with whom he was placed in the identification parade were all quite obviously British. In addition
to this, thanks to the attention the press had given to
the case, the witnesses had all had a chance to have a
good look at Slater's photograph in the paper. They
were probably well prepared to identify someone who
looked like the photograph in the paper rather than
the man they claimed to have seen hanging around
Marion Gilchrist's house – if they had seen a man at
all. Could there have been any possibility of any of the
witnesses pointing to the wrong man and announcing:
'That's him!'?

The Trial

And so to the trial, which took place in Edinburgh, beginning on 3 May 1909. The people had waited a long time for this. By now the tide of opinion had well and truly turned against Slater. In theory he should have been presumed innocent until proven guilty. In reality, Oscar Slater's defence team found themselves facing an uphill task trying to prove that he was innocent. He was, quite definitely, assumed to be guilty. Whatever doubts the prosecution lawyers had about the strength of their case against Oscar Slater, they did not show them in court. The man appearing for the prosecution was none other than the Lord Advocate himself, Alexander Ure. A skilful and persuasive advocate, he was determined to get his man, by fair means or foul.

Mr A. McClure, appearing for Slater, did a good job as far as it went, but he omitted to bring up certain points that were crucial to the case. Firstly, Oscar Slater had an alibi for the night of the murder. Miss Gilchrist had been killed at around seven o'clock in the evening. At that time, according to both Slater's mistress and his maid, Slater had returned home, as he usually did, to eat dinner. He had stayed at home for more than an hour. He had witnesses who testified to his presence in various places during the afternoon before the murder. His last port of call had been a billiard hall in Renfield Street. He had left there at six-thirty. The prosecution claimed that it was at this point that Slater had gone to Miss

Gilchrist's flat, killed her and then returned home by a very circuitous route, arriving at his flat hours later than usual. Had the defence been more efficient, they would surely have protested against this proposition. There was no time for Oscar to race all the way to Miss Gilchrist's, kill her and arrive home in time for seven o'clock. And there were witnesses who said he was home by seven o'clock. In fact, from the billiard room in Renfield Street, it was virtually impossible for Oscar to have got to Miss Gilchrist's in time to kill her. The prosecution's propositions made no real sense; they were not backed up by evidence of any sort. They were pure conjecture, but they were put with such persuasion that they won the day.

Again, the defence was to let Slater down when it came to the hours immediately after Miss Gilchrist's death. Slater had witnesses to say that he had come home for dinner. Their statements were virtually overlooked in the judge's summing up of the case. The defence plainly did not give enough weight to their statements when presenting its case – either that or the judge felt that they had been lying.

If the defence lawyers had researched the case a little more thoroughly, they might have found out about another witness, one whom the prosecution knew about, but chose not to call to give evidence for obvious reasons. This witness was a grocer to whom Oscar Slater was familiar as a customer. He saw Oscar Slater standing at the entrance to his close, smoking a cigar in a calm and relaxed fashion, at about eight-fifteen on the night of the murder. Slater certainly did not have the appearance of a man who had committed a hasty and brutal murder only an hour earlier. The grocer's statement never came to the attention of the defence and was never brought up in court. It might have saved Oscar Slater.

If we recall how security conscious the late Miss Gilchrist was, then we will be surprised that nothing was made of the fact that the means by which Oscar was supposed to have gained entry to her flat remained a mystery. The police had been convinced that she must have known her assailant. There had been no forced entry and Miss Gilchrist would never have opened her door to a stranger. This appears to have been conveniently overlooked from the moment the police fixed their attentions on Oscar Slater. The prosecution did not give any explanation as to how Slater was supposed to have become familiar with Miss Gilchrist and gained access to her home. They concentrated their line of attack on the fact that they had several witnesses who could attest to Slater's presence in the area, lurking suspiciously, in the days leading up to the murder.

Once again, the case for the prosecution did not make much sense. The Lord Advocate was very eloquent in his description of Slater, lurking, watching, making a mental note of the regular movements of the two women in Miss Gilchrist's flat. He knew when to strike.

But if this was the case, why had Oscar chosen a moment when he had only minutes to carry out the terrible deed? If he had been 'casing the joint', he would know that Nellie's trip was bound to be a short one – her usual outing to get the evening paper. If he really had been watching Miss Gilchrist's flat for as long as the prosecution claimed, then he would surely know that there were better moments to pick when he would have more time. Nellie Lambie had time off twice a week, during which she always went out. Why did Oscar not act then? Nobody asked this question.

Then there was the question of the murder weapon. Dr Adams, arriving at the scene of the murder, had declared that a chair had been used to kill Miss Gilchrist. This fact was completely overlooked when the police found the hammer in Oscar Slater's luggage. The hammer was stained and the police decided that the stains could be blood; they were, in fact, rust. But the hammer was still supposed to be the murder weapon. Dr Adams was never called to give evidence as to his findings.

Finally, there was Oscar Slater's supposed motive – a need for money. This made little sense. Oscar had enough money for his trip to the United States and he was not short of cash either. The brooch that he had pawned – the brooch that had started off the whole dismal affair – had earned him £30. He had work waiting for him in the United States. He had no need to rob Miss Gilchrist. Besides, apart from the brooch that was missing, the brooch that Oscar Slater had clearly not taken, nothing had gone from Miss Gilchrist's home. There had been plenty of valuable items lying within easy reach, items that could have been grabbed as the killer made his hasty exit, but nothing else had been taken.

The Lord Advocate was determined to have Oscar Slater found guilty and although the evidence upon which he based his case was decidedly shaky to say the least, the power of his rhetoric concealed the weaknesses in his arguments well enough to convince most of the jury. The judge, Lord Guthrie, appeared to have been convinced as well. His summing up of the case made his opinion perfectly clear. He condemned Oscar Slater as a fundamentally dishonest person of unsavoury character. He ignored the alibi that Madame Junio Antoine and Oscar's maid had given him for the evening of the murder. In short, Lord Guthrie ensured that Oscar Slater's fate was sealed.

The verdict was not unanimous. Nine found Slater guilty, five found the case against him not proven, one found him innocent. The conviction had been secured by a narrow majority, but it was enough to win the case for the prosecution. Oscar Slater was pronounced guilty as charged and sentenced to death. His dismay at the court's findings was obvious for all to see. He had not been permitted to take the stand in his own defence in case his foreign accent prejudiced his case. Now he would not be silenced. He stood up in court after the verdict had been announced and protested his innocence most forcefully. Whether this made him feel any better, we do not know. It certainly did not help him. He was to be hanged on 27 May 1909.

Immediately after the trial, the tide of public opinion began to shift in Oscar Slater's favour. Some twenty thousand people gave their names to a petition calling for the death sentence to be commuted. The petition argued two main points. First, it stated that Oscar Slater's character ought not to have been called into question in the way it was by the judge before the jury reached their verdict. This had prejudiced his case. Secondly, the identification of Oscar Slater had been most unsatisfactory.

Two days before he was due to be hanged, the terrified and bewildered Oscar Slater found that his sentence had been commuted to life imprisonment. He was transferred to Peterhead Prison. From there he continued to protest his innocence at every opportunity. He believed that someone, somewhere, would be able to help him. His words in a letter to Mr Shaughnessy, the lawyer whom he engaged to help him, showed that in spite of everything he still had faith that justice would win the day:

'I will fight so long as I live in here, I am not crying to get liberated, I want justice and this I will get at last.'

There were several people on Slater's side. One of Oscar's supporters was the great Arthur Conan Doyle, who published a book on the case in August 1912. He felt that a crucial point overlooked in the investigation was the rifled box of papers in Miss Gilchrist's flat. He believed that the papers – in particular a will – held the reason for the murder. Sir Edward Marshall Hall brought the matter up in parliament, asking the Scottish Secretary to act. The Scottish Secretary did nothing.

It was fortunate for Oscar Slater that there was one man in the Glasgow police force who felt very strongly that justice had not been done. Detective-Lieutenant John Trench, who had been involved in the case from the outset, was deeply disturbed. From the very first day of the murder investigation, Trench had been given every reason to believe that Nellie Lambie had known the intruder in Miss Gilchrist's flat.

Trench had been silenced in his protestations to his superiors at the time as they were hot in pursuit of Oscar Slater, but the affair did not sit easily on his conscience. Then in 1912 Trench had become involved in another case that had borne remarkable similarities to the Gilchrist case. An elderly spinster had been murdered in her home in Broughty Ferry, and by means that could only be described as dubious the police had found several witnesses to identify a Canadian man as the likely culprit. It had been Trench who had put in the effort and the real detective work to prove that this man was entirely innocent. As he worked on the Broughty Ferry case, the Gilchrist case can never have been far from his mind. Slater's unfortunate predicament troubled him more and more.

Trench was in a difficult position. He was putting his own career at risk, calling the actions of his own police force into question, but he felt strongly that his moral duty was to speak up. He told his story to a lawyer, David Cook, and asked for his help. Through David Cook, Trench's concerns reached the ears of the Scottish Secretary. At the Scottish Secretary's request, Trench supplied him with a long and detailed document containing the information that he felt was vital to the Slater case. This move was backed up by a plea, made in March 1914 by David Cook, for the Scottish Secretary to open an inquiry into the case.

Finally the inquiry was arranged and Trench had his turn to speak. His concerns about the case were several:

1   He believed that Nellie Lambie had recognised the intruder in her mistress's flat on the night of the murder. He claimed that the police had been told the name of the man whom Nellie Lambie believed it to have been and it was not Oscar Slater.

2   He thought that the statement of Mary Barrowman, and her description of the man she claimed to have seen on the night of the murder was pure fabrication. Barrowman had said that she was in West Princes Street on an errand on the night in question, but her employers had denied this.

3   Oscar Slater's supposed flight from justice gave cause for concern. There was remarkably little evidence to suggest that he had left in a great hurry. Moreover, upon his arrival in Liverpool he

had quite openly signed his name in the hotel register as 'Oscar Slater, Glasgow'. Oscar Slater had never hesitated to use false names in the past. If he really was on the run, then why had he chosen to use his own name now, of all times? Moreover, Oscar's eventual destination, New York, and the means by which he was travelling, on board the Lusitania, were never a secret.

4 The matches found on the table below the gas lamp in the spare bedroom in Miss Gilchrist's house were Runaway matches. This was a brand that Miss Gilchrist did not use and the box was supposed to have been left by the killer. When Trench went to search Oscar Slater's flat he found no evidence to suggest that this particular brand of matches was used in the Slater residence either.

The most important point that Trench made concerned Nellie Lambie's supposed identification of the intruder. Trench was most insistent about this, and it cost him his job, for he was calling into question the evidence of his superiors.

Trench had become involved in the case when Central Division, to which he belonged, was called in to help Western Division. One of the first pieces of information he was given about the case was the description of the wanted man that had been supplied by Arthur Adams and Nellie Lambie.

On 22 December, Trench knew that three police

officers, including Superintendent Douglas, had visited the house of a man known as A. B., following up some information that Nellie Lambie had given them.

On 23 December, Trench had gone, at the request of Chief Superintendent Orr, to take a statement from Miss Birrel, 19 Blythswood Drive. Miss Birrel was Miss Gilchrist's niece, and Nellie Lambie had visited her on the night of the murder to tell her of her aunt's death. Miss Birrel told Trench that Nellie Lambie had stated, quite categorically, that A. B. had been the man she had seen in the flat. A. B., according to Nellie Lambie, had been the murderer. Miss Birrel also said that Nellie Lambie had told the police about A. B.

Upon his return to headquarters with this information, Trench had been congratulated. According to Chief Superintendent Orr, it was 'the first real clue we have got'. Superintendent Ord was present with his superior, Orr, when Trench passed on the information. Shortly after that, Ord told Trench that he had consulted Superintendent Douglas, who was convinced that A. B. had nothing to do with the affair.

Trench had been less convinced. He visited Nellie Lambie at her aunt's house on 3 January, accompanied by Detective Keith. He showed a sketch of Oscar Slater to her, but she did not recognise him. Trench then mentioned A. B. Was that possibly the man whom she saw? Nellie's reply was: 'It's gey funny if it wasn't him I saw!' Trench then went back to Ord with this information but was more or less ignored. The intruder was not A. B., according to Ord. The matter had been 'cleared up'.

Trench's theory that Nellie Lambie had known the identity of the intruder and that the intruder had been A. B. made a great deal of sense. It explained why Nellie had shown no apparent dismay at the man's appearance. It also explained how the man had gained entry to the flat. A. B. was known both to Nellie Lambie and Miss Gilchrist.

When fellow officers in Central Division and Western Division were questioned at the inquiry, however, they were adamant to a man that Trench was not telling the truth. Trench had a copy of the statement made by Miss Birrel on 23 December, but, strangely, such a statement was missing from the file held by Superintendent Ord. Detective Keith denied that Trench had ever mentioned A. B. to Nellie Lambie on 9 January. And so it went on. If the Glasgow police had realised that their investig-ation was a foul-up, they certainly were not going to admit it. To add to Trench's misery, Nellie Lambie and Miss Birrel, when questioned again, denied the whole story of the mysterious A. B. The whole inquiry was a farce. It benefited Oscar Slater not one bit.

Detective-Lieutenant John Trench was suspended from duty on 14 July. His conscience had cost him his career.

In early August, war broke out and there were other things on the minds of the government and the great British public. Oscar Slater was left to languish in jail.

For Trench and Cook, the lawyer who had helped him, things were getting worse. In May 1915, both men were arrested separately on similar charges of reset. The crime had supposedly taken place in January 1914. The whole affair was clearly a set-up, with the police behind it, and luckily Trench and Cook were acquitted, but the whole affair had left them with a very bad taste in their mouths.

It was now abundantly clear that Trench could take the Slater case no further personally. He had taken up a career in the army and now he went to serve abroad.

Slater, amazingly, had still not given up hope. The years went by – five, ten, fifteen – still he was not released, but he was still convinced that justice would eventually be done. In early 1925, he made contact with a man he knew to be an ally from the past, Sir Arthur Conan Doyle, and begged him to try again on his behalf.

Conan Doyle approached the Secretary of State for Scotland and asked him to consider the case as Oscar Slater had already served more than fifteen years, the usual length of a life sentence at that time.

Sir Herbert Stephen, a prominent figure in English legal circles, took up arms on behalf of Slater as well, publishing an article decrying the manner in which Slater had been convicted and stating, most provocatively, that such a thing would never have happened in England.

John Trench was by now dead. He had died in 1919, age fifty, but his influence on the Slater case had not died with him. Trench had told a journalist friend the whole story before he left for foreign fields. The journalist was a man called William Park. In 1927, Park published a book, entitled *The Truth About Oscar Slater*, that was to cause a sensation. The book contained every single detail supplied to him by Trench, including Trench's theory about what had really happened on the night of Miss Gilchrist's death.

All hell broke loose. The newspapers were full of it. The Scottish legal system was held up to mockery. Statements supposedly from Nellie Lambie and Mary Barrowman were published in the press. Public pressure mounted. Oscar Slater should be released.

Gradually the pressure forced Sir John Gilmour, the Secretary of State for Scotland, to cave in. Oscar Slater was released from prison on licence but not granted a pardon on 14 November 1927, after eighteen-and-a-half years in prison.

Oscar Slater and his supporters had not finished yet. Led by the indomitable Conan Doyle, they pressed for an inquiry into the case. Sir John Gilmour knew he had no choice but to agree. On 8 June 1928, the appeal before the recently constituted Court of Criminal Appeal began in Edinburgh.

Slater was represented by Craigie Aitchison KC, who had done an admirable job in the past twelve months, gathering piles of evidence from witnesses and studying the statements and evidence that had been brought to court in 1909. Oscar himself was not to be called as a witness, and this caused him considerable anxiety. The last time this happened, things had gone very much against him. But his defence counsel was adamant.

Mr Craigie Aitchison was quite brilliant and very thorough. He punched holes in the Lord Advocate's case for the prosecution against Oscar Slater with consummate ease. He also condemned, quite unequivocally, the manner in which the character of Slater had been assassinated by the prosecution. This had undoubtedly biased his client's case. Finally, he was very critical of the conduct of Lord Guthrie, the judge in the Slater trial. In his final address, Lord Guthrie had denied Oscar Slater 'the full benefit of the presumption of innocence'.

Slater's conviction was quashed.

OUTCOME

The story does have a happy ending, but the beginning was tragic and the middle should never be forgotten. It was a catalogue of catastrophic misdirection and prejudiced investigation. Oscar Slater was innocent, but while he languished in jail for nearly nineteen years, somewhere a killer walked free.

CHAPTER 13
Helen Duncan (1944)

*'Helen Duncan, Ernest Edward Hartland Homer,
Elizabeth Anne Jones and Frances Brown, you four
are charged with an indictment that contains seven
counts. In the first count that between 1 December
1943 and 19 January 1944 you conspired together
and with other persons unknown to pretend to
exercise or use a kind of conjuration, to wit, that
through the agency of the said Helen Duncan spirits
of deceased persons should appear to be present in fact
in such place as the said Helen Duncan was then
in, and that the said spirits were communicating
with living persons then and there present contrary
to Section 4 of the Witchcraft Act 1735.'*

The last person to be accused and convicted under the
Witchcraft Act of 1735 was a Scottish woman, Helen
Duncan, in 1944. She wasn't a witch, of course, but a
medium. The Act itself had antecedents in the 1604
Witchcraft Act, brought in by James VI of Scotland
and I of England, that declared death was the penalty
for anyone 'conjuring diabolic spirits'. By 1735, offend-
ers were punished by being exposed to public ridicule
and scorn in a pillory.

Helen Duncan wasn't sentenced to drowning or burning or being placed in a pillory for her crimes of witchcraft, but her arrest and trial would take a toll on her health. Many of her friends and supporters were outraged that an innocent woman was being persecuted for witchcraft while others believed there was some sort of government conspiracy against Helen fed by the suspicions and scaremongering of wartime. There is little doubt that Duncan was to a large extent the victim of over-zealous authorities, but many would argue she had benefited from the despair of those who had lost loved ones. Whether she was a victim, or a con woman, does she deserves the title of 'the last woman in Britain to be found 'guilty' of witchcraft'?

BACKGROUND

Helen Duncan was born Victoria Helen MacFarlane on 25 November 1897 in Callander, a small town bordering an area of outstanding natural beauty in Scotland known as 'the Trossachs'. She was the fourth of eight children, born to a slater father, Archie, and his wife, Isabella. Known as Nell from early childhood, she always maintained that she was aware of having 'psychic gifts' from the age of about seven. When she was fourteen years old, the First World War broke out and she was later to claim that she had predicted the war would last years and not weeks.

Helen fell pregnant at a young age but the father

of her baby was never named and she was sent off in disgrace to Dundee where she gave birth to her first child. As a young unmarried mother, the prospects for the rest of her life did not, at this point, look very good at all. However, by great good fortune, she met Henry Duncan that year. A soldier from Dundee who had been invalided out of the army with rheumatic fever, he fell in love with her straightaway. They married the following year and Helen must have been relieved at receiving an offer of marriage when she already had one fatherless child. She and Henry went on to have a large family – she gave birth to eight children in total (Bella, her first and illegitimate child by another man, Nan, Henrietta, Lilian, Gena, Peter and Henry), although two (Alex and Etta) would not survive childhood.

Both parents suffered regular bouts of ill health. Henry had a nervous breakdown and then a heart attack, no doubt as a result of his experiences during the First World War. Helen was overweight and so much child-bearing had also given her back pain so severe that she would often faint. They were not wealthy but when Helen started to give psychic readings, their financial situation improved dramatically. Henry, who was in effect Helen's manager, must have realised the lucrative possibilities of his wife's 'gift' early on.

The First World War had seen a huge surge in the popularity of spiritualism and séances; many people had lost loved ones and some in their despair clung to the belief that they could be contacted in the afterlife.

Psychics and mediums were suddenly in huge demand. Famous followers and advocates of spiritualism included Arthur Conan Doyle who had lost a son just before the end of the First World War. (Writer, Vera Brittain, on the other hand recorded in her memoir, *Testament of Youth*, that she lost her belief in God because both her fiancé and her brother, who had promised to contact her somehow from the afterlife if they were killed, had not done so.)

Helen began to conduct séances as a classic 'materialisation medium'. She went much further than merely contacting spirits during her performance. She produced ectoplasm (a milky substance that could give life to spirit forms) from her mouth. According to her daughter, the ectoplasm Helen produced was 'a substance not unlike cheesecloth or butter muslin'. She also had a couple of regular 'ghosts', a tall Scotsman called Albert and a young girl called Peggy, who would regularly appear before those attending her séances.

Malcolm Gaskill, in his book *Hellish Nell: Last of Britain's Witches*, tells us that 'Helen Duncan's reputation grew in the early 1930s as more people fell under the spell of spiritualism and sought the kind of mediumship at which she excelled.' He writes that she was regarded as 'a coarse, gross fish-wifey' and being so overweight made regular fainting fits from drops in her blood-sugar level common. The sight of ectoplasm or anything else coming out of this huge body, must have been quite intimidating.

Her success meant that Helen was now travelling regularly throughout Britain to 'perform' her séances. As her fame continued to grow, the London Spiritualist Alliance contracted her to hold séances for them in London but these séances were also test séances as the Alliance were keen to expose fraudulent mediums. Helen and Henry must have found them quite challenging!

As Gaskill notes, doubts about the authenticity of supernatural beings during séances were beginning to circulate – 'fleshy arms' beneath a ghostly figure were detected, and some spirit babies looked remarkably like dolls. There was a growing need to establish the truth about what Helen was doing. The Society for Psychical Research, for example, took their business very seriously indeed, and liked to root out imposters. One of their investigators, Harry Price, had split off from the Society in 1923 and founded the National Laboratory of Psychical Research. The first time Helen encountered Price was when she was being observed by him at the Laboratory. She got hysterical during the examination and ran out into the street screaming. Price eventually wrote a piece about Helen, suggesting she was faking her entire business.

The Duncans hit back at these accusations, and Helen went on to obtain a diploma at the Edinburgh Psychic College. However, one séance went disastrously wrong, as Gaskill recounts: a Miss Esson Maule had asked Helen to conduct a séance at her house in Edinburgh, at which she grabbed Peggy, the little 'child ghost', and found she was made from solid material. Helen refused to remove her clothing so that Maule could inspect her, and in the ensuing chaos threw a chair at her. The police were called and Helen was charged with criminal fraud. She pled 'not guilty', but the case went against her and she was fined £10. She now had a criminal record, and this would cause serious problems for her when she later appeared in court for a second time. Gaskill does note, however, that being found 'guilty' of fraud did little to harm Helen's career – on the contrary, it painted her as a martyr. Newspapers interviewed her and carried articles by her. In 1933, he writes:

> 'Helen was applauded at public meetings, includ-
> ing one where she established clairvoyantly that a
> man in the audience had brought along his wife's
> ashes in a tea caddy.'

At the start of the Second World War, mediums found themselves in greater demand than ever – could they tell how long this war would last? Could they predict who would live and who would die? Gaskill writes that by 1944 there were reckoned to be at least a million followers of spiritualism, and, of all the mediums, Helen was the most well-known. As Gaskill points out, she spent 'most of her time in places where the need for her services was greatest' and that meant port towns like Portsmouth.

At a séance held by Helen in the Psychic Centre in

Portsmouth, shortly after the sinking of HMS *Barham* –
a battleship destroyed by the Germans on 25 November
1944 in which 841 souls perished – the spirit of one of
the dead sailors on board appeared to his mother. The
problem was that the War Office hadn't released any
news of this disaster for the sake of British morale and
to confuse the Germans. The naval authorities became
interested in Duncan after the sailor's mother called
the Admiralty for confirmation of the ship's destruction.
When she was asked how she had come by such classi-
fied information, she told them about Helen Duncan's
séance.

In 1944, Helen was hauled up in front of the courts
again on more fraud charges but was bailed. The authorities then decided to pursue a more serious charge of
conspiracy to defraud, and in February, Helen was
formally charged. For various reasons, her case was
moved from Portsmouth to the Old Bailey in London,
and prosecutors felt they needed something stronger
to make the case against her stick. They came up with
Section 4 of the 1735 Witchcraft Act.

Trial

The trial took place on 23 March 1944 at the Old Bailey
in London. Charged alongside her for conspiracy to
contravene this Act were Ernest and Elizabeth Homer,
who operated the Psychic Centre in Portsmouth, and
Frances Brown, Helen's agent who went with her to

set up her séances. Forty-five defence witnesses would be called. According to Gaskill, the prosecution's case rested on proving not that Helen was an imposter, but that she had pretended to conjure up the spirits of the dead. A series of séances were recalled at which it was alleged by the prosecution that Helen simply put a sheet over her head. Clearly, it was suggested, things could have been hidden on Helen's clothing, or even in the rooms that she used. For the defence, witnesses testified to seeing, or hearing from, dead relatives at these séances, and that on one occasion Mary, Queen of Scots, had passed on messages. To some, it seemed as though spiritualism itself was on trial. Helen's defence counsel asked for her to be allowed to conduct a séance in court, but this request was turned down.

Even though many of Helen's supporters were very respectable, like the RAF wing commander who testified to seeing his dead mother, there was a sense, according to Gaskill, that 'the repetitiveness of the stories, however marvellous and poignant, [were] eating away at the roots of the Recorder's tolerance.' Receipts were examined and the texture of the ectoplasm said to have been produced at these séances was investigated, although many testified to seeing ectoplasm that wasn't like cloth at all.

Helen's previous conviction was disclosed (after much discussion about whether this disclosure was legal or not). It was probably the one piece of evidence that sank her case. Gaskill quotes a Spiritualists' National Union (SNU) official, Percy Wilson, describing what happened after this fifth day in court, when Helen was staying at his house:

> '... and then upstairs to the séance room ... I have never seen such a mass of ectoplasm. It bundled up on her bosom, dropped to the floor and then jumped up to her hand.'

Medical officers and psychic investigators proceeded to give evidence in Helen's favour but it was no use. Even a friend of Arthur Conan Doyle, Sir James Herries, couldn't convince the jury. That night, she predicted 'two will be convicted and two will go free.' All the charges were dropped apart from the conspiracy to contravene the Witchcraft Act. The prosecutor called on the jury to disbelieve the fantastical elements of the séances, to dispute any authenticity of those spirits who were said to have appeared. When the jury delivered their verdict, after only twenty-four minutes, they found all four defendants 'guilty'. Helen's prediction of the night before had not even been correct.

She was subsequently sentenced to nine months' imprisonment: the jurors did not believe the testimonies of those who professed to see ectoplasm come out of her mouth, or that she really did conjure up the spirits of the dead (in that sense, she wasn't quite within the definition of the act). They thought she pretended to do so. Should she really have been prosecuted at all then?

It was one of the chef constables in the case who

noted, as Gaskill highlights, that she had 'transgressed the security laws, again in a naval connection, when she foretold of the loss of one of His Majesty's ships long before the fact was made public.' Was that the real reason she was prosecuted?

Helen was taken away to Holloway Prison and the newspapers had a field day, both with the trial and the conviction. But how had she known about the sinking of the *Barham*? Gaskill writes that the easiest explanation is that 'the prediction was never made – or at least, not in the way described in the canonical version.' He argues that it was common knowledge that the Barham had:

> 'already been torpedoed off the coast of Scotland in December 1939 and bombed during the with-drawal from Crete in 1941. At the séance attended by Brigadier Firebrace, the prediction concerned only a "great British battleship" and was made during the protracted Battle of the Atlantic, costly from early on in the war when HMS *Courageous* and the battleship *Royal Oak* had been sunk.'

Helen had some supporters in high places – Gaskill quotes a letter from Winston Churchill, where he asks for a report into the reasons for charging her under the Witchcraft Act, and how much all this 'obsolete tom-foolery' had cost the state, but he disputes that Churchill ever visited Helen in prison.

CONCLUSION

On 8 June1944, Helen's appeal against her sentence was heard. But after eleven days, her conviction was upheld. The SNU kept campaigning for her release, as did many of her supporters, but she was finally released after serving more than half her sentence.

Her trial and conviction under the Witchcraft Act didn't change her ways. After her release from prison, Helen carried on as a medium, conducting séances in both England and Scotland, and on one occasion even in Paris. In 1951, the Witchcraft Act was repealed. Five years later, Helen died, worn out, probably, with repeated regurgitations of her kind of ectoplasm and the stress of regular, sometimes nightly, séances. The two trials she had been forced to appear in, and her stay in Holloway, would also not have helped the health of a woman who was grossly overweight. Her husband, Henry, died eleven years later.

Was Helen Duncan innocent or was she guilty? Did she pretend or did she really conjure up the spirits of the dead? Gaskill sees her as an imposter, which makes her conviction under the Witchcraft Act actually more, not less, ludicrous. The 'last witch in Britain' wasn't even a medium, you might argue, far less a witch. Her conviction is still the focus of a sustained campaign to have it overturned.

Bibliography

City of Glasgow Bank 'The Trial of the City of Glasgow
  Bank Directors' (*Notable Scottish Trials*, 1905)

Earl of Birkenhead *Famous Trials of History* (Garden
  City of Publishing, 1926)

Flanders, Judith *The Invention of Murder: How the
  Victorians Revelled in Death and Detection and
  Created Modern Crime* (Harper Press, 2011)

Gaskill, Malcolm *Hellish Nell: The Last of Britain's
  Witches* (Fourth Estate, 2001)

Gordon, Eleanor and Nair, Gwyneth *Murder and
  Morality in Victorian Britain: The Story of Madeleine
  Smith* (Manchester University Press, 2009)

Guy, John *My Heart is My Own: The Life of Mary,
  Queen of Scots* (Harper Perennial, 2004)

High Court Justiciary 'The Trial of William Burke and
  Helen McDougal' (1829)

High Court Justiciary 'The Trial of Thomas Muir' (1794)

Lockyer, Roger (editor) 'The Trial of Charles I' (Folio
  Society, 1959)

Marshall, Rosalind K. *Mary Queen of Scots: Truth or
  Lies* (St Andrews Press, 2011)

Roughead, William (editor) 'The Trial of Mrs McLachlan'
  (*Notable Scottish Trials* series, 1911)

Roughead, William (editor) 'The Trial of Deacon Brodie'
  (*Notable Scottish Trials,* 1906)

Sinclair, David 'The Land That Never Was: Sir Gregor McGregor and the most audacious fraud in history' (*Scottish Historical Review*, vol. 85, no.2 2006)

Smith, A. Duncan 'The Trial of Madeleine Smith' (*Notable Scottish Trials*, 1905)

Weir, Alison *Mary Queen of Scots and the Murder of Lord Darnley* (Vintage, 2003)

Hamilton, Judy *Scottish Murders* (Waverley Books, 2009)